Fort Collins Area Trails

A Guide To Trails Within 25 Miles Of Fort Collins, Colorado

By

John E. Heasley

RAS Publishing

Shedding light on the great outdoors

2917 Eagle Drive, Fort Collins, Colorado 80526

www.resourceanalysis.com

RAS Publishing, 2917 Eagle Drive, Fort Collins, CO 80526

Printed in the United States of America

Photos and maps by the author

Book design by Resource Analysis Systems, Ft. Collins, CO

970 - 226- 2311   www.resourceanalysis.com

08 07 06 05 04   54321

Library of Congress Catalog Card Number: 2004095544

ISBN: 0-9671040-2-5

Disclaimer

This book contains information gathered from many sources. Every effort has been made to ensure the accuracy of this information. This book is published for general reference and not as a substitute for independent verification by users when circumstances warrant. The publisher and author will not be held responsible for any inconvenience or injury resulting from the use or misuse of the maps, diagrams, or text of this book.

Contents

Introduction.. 9

   Trail Rules and Etiquette............................ 10

   Trail Data 11

   Trail Summary 12

Besant Point 17

Black Powder 21

   Overlook 24

Coyote Ridge 25

Devil's Backbone 29

Fawn Hollow.. 33

Foothills 37

Fossil Creek 41

Greyrock 45

Hewlett Gulch 49

Horsetooth Mountain Park 53

   Audra Culver....................................... 56

   Carey Springs...................................... 59

Herrington 61

Horsetooth Falls 64

Horsetooth Rock 67

Loggers 70

Mill Creek 73

Nomad 76

Sawmill 79

Soderberg 82

Spring Creek 85

Stout 88

Wathen 91

Westridge 94

Lory State Park 97

Arthur's Rock 100

East Valley 103

Mill Creek Link 106

Overlook 109

Shoreline 112

South Valley 115

Timber 118

Waterfall 121

Well Gulch 124

Westridge 127

West Valley 130

Loveland Recreation 133

Pineridge Natureal Area 137

Park 138

Reservoir 140

Ridge 138

South Loop 138

Timber 138

Valley 138

Viewpoint 140

Pleasant Valley 141

Poudre River (Fort Collins) 145

Poudre River (Windsor) 149

Power 153

Round Mountain 157

Shoshone 161

Spring Creek 165

Sundance 169

Young Gulch 173

Index 177

CD ROM 179

About The Author

 John Heasley has been hiking, camping, and fishing in Colorado for over 25 years. Since he received his PhD in ecology in 1978, John has been actively involved in the application of technologies to natural resource problems. He has worked for Colorado State University, the US Fish and Wildlife Service, and the US Forest Service. He founded Resource Analysis Systems in 1988. RAS is dedicated to the development and application of new technologies for the collection and analysis of information concerning our use of the natural environment.

In 1994, John developed software for the generation of 3D trail maps for several wilderness areas in northern Colorado and Rocky Mountain National Park. These maps help the hiker to better visualize the terrain and the lay of the land. A lot of information has been collected about natural resources that is not readily available to people who love the outdoors. John hopes to change that by using technology to bring you truly useful information through the publication of books, maps, CD's, and making detailed information about Colorado's outdoor resources available on-line. John has also written "Colorado Campgrounds: Volume 1", a book providing detailed descriptions of northern Colorado campgrounds, "Colorado's Indian Peaks Wilderness--A Guide To Trails And Lakes", and "Leaving The Crowds Behind--A GuideTo Backcountry Camping In Rocky Mountain National Park. He also produced "Rocky Mountain Trails", a CD covering 111 trails in Rocky Mountain National Park.

Acknowledgment

I would like to thank all of the park and city personnel for providing information on trails and rules for their use. Thanks go to John Messineo for taking the author's photo. As always a special thanks goes to my wife Linda, for reading the manuscript and providing helpful suggestions and without whose support this book would not have been possible.

Introduction

Fort Collins, Colorado, located about 65 miles northwest of Denver, lies in the shadow of the foothills of the Rocky Mountains. It has a population of over 126,000, many of whom are avid enthusiasts of outdoor activities. Some of these activities include: walking/hiking, running, roller blading, biking, and horseback riding. The climate of this area is characterized by moderate temperatures, light winds, and light precipitation. This type of climate offers year round opportunities for getting outside and enjoying these activities. Although there are hundreds of opportunities for hiking, biking, and horseback riding within a hundred mile radius of Fort Collins, many of these locations require several hours to reach. The busy lifestyles of people living in the Fort Collins area, including Loveland and Windsor, do not allow the luxury of driving to the mountains frequently to enjoy their outdoor pursuits. This book is a comprehensive guide to trails within 25 miles of Fort Collins that offer a variety of possibilities for frequent enjoyment of the great outdoors.

There are 52 trails within a 25 mile radius of Fort Collins. They range in length from .04 miles to 10.35 miles, totaling over 131 miles. Most of the trails feature a natural surface, dirt or rock. Seven of the trails are paved, concrete or asphalt. Some are within walking distance of many neighborhoods while others are a half hour to forty minutes away. They range in elevation from 4,700 feet to almost 8,500 feet above sea level. Twenty four of the trails are easy to hike, fourteen are easy to moderate, and fourteen are moderate in difficulty. All of the trails are suitable for walking/hiking or running. Forty three are suitable for bicyclists or mountain biking. Horseback riding is permitted on thirty nine of the trails in the Fort Collins area. Whether you are interested in a simple stroll, a bicycle ride in a serene setting, a place to ride your horse, or a demanding mountain bike ride or hike, the Fort Collins area has your trails.

Trail Rules and Etiquette

The trails in this book are maintained by the cities of Fort Collins and Loveland, Larimer County Parks and Recreation, or Colorado State Parks. Pets are permitted on all of the trails with the exception of Coyote Ridge. All pets must be controlled by a leash of six to ten feet maximum length. Firearms, fireworks, and hunting are not allowed on most trails within this area. Lory State Park does permit hunting in restricted areas. Motorized vehicles are not allowed on most of the trails. Open fires are not permitted outside of designated fire pits and grates. Alcoholic beverages and glass containers are generally not permitted on most trails. Most trails are day use only trails and do not allow overnight camping. Overnight camping is permitted, however, in the Horsetooth Mountain Park backcountry and at six designated camping sites in Lory State Park. The city of Fort Collins trails are closed between 11 pm and 5 am. Where trails can be used for different types of recreation (hiking, biking, and horseback riding), bikers should yield to hikers and horses and hikers should yield to horses.

Many of the trails in the Fort Collins area receive moderate to high use. In order to avoid conflict with other users and to ensure an enjoyable trail experience for everyone, the following guidelines for trail etiquette should be followed:

- Stay to the right side of the trail when the trail is wide.

- Groups should hike or ride single file.

- Slow down when overtaking or meeting other trail users. Warn others that you are passing from behind.

- Hikers, bicyclists, and skaters should yield to horses. Bicyclists should yield to hikers and skaters. Skaters should yield to hikers.

- Do not disturb wildlife. View them from a distance.

- Leave wildflowers for others to enjoy.

- Stay on the trail. Do not cut across switchbacks.

- Be courteous to all trail users.

- Respect private property.

Trail Data

Each of the trails in this book has been mapped using Global Positioning System satellites. The position of each trail has been determined to an accuracy of 2 - 5 meters. Trail maps were created using this data. Altitude profiles were generated for each trail using the trail position data and USGS Digital Elevation Model data. Elevation gains and losses are

Trail Summary Table

Trail	Length one way	Elevation	Difficulty
Arthur's Rock	1.69 mi	5,644' - 6,716'	Moderate
Audra Culver	.67 mi	6,680'-6,975'	Moderate
Besant Point	2.26 mi	6,569' - 6,609'	Easy
Black Powder	.63 mi	5,395' - 5,792'	Moderate
Carey Springs	.24 mi	6,291' - 6,333'	Easy
Coyote Ridge	3.71 mi	5,125' - 5,643'	Easy to moderate
Devil's Backbone	3.56 mi	5,069' - 5,518'	Easy to moderate
East Valley	2.02 mi	5,433' - 5,621'	Easy
Fawn Hollow	.73 mi	5,760' - 5,924'	Easy to moderate
Foothills	6.07 mi	5,136' - 5,698'	Easy to moderate
Fossil Creek	2.39 mi	5,006' - 5,141'	Easy
Greyrock	3.16 - 4.46 mi	5,581' - 7,611'	Moderate
Herrington	.80 mi	6,229' - 6,464'	Moderate
Hewlett Gulch	5.70 mi	5,667' - 6,780'	Easy to moderate
Horsetooth Falls	.82 mi	5,733' - 5,903'	Easy to moderate
Horsetooth Rock	1.25 mi	6,193' - 6,940'	Moderate
Loggers	1.28 mi	6,090' - 6,281'	Easy to moderate
Loveland Recreation	10.35 mi	4,917' - 4,989'	Easy
Mill Creek	2.91 mi	5,853'-6,918'	Moderate
Mill Creek Link	.77 mi	5,622' - 5,972'	Moderate
Nomad	1.04 mi	5,488' - 5,568'	Easy
Overlook (Lory)	1.15 mi	5,832' - 6,122'	Moderate
Overlook (Gateway)	.25 mi	5,402' - 5,537'	Easy

Trail	Surface	Suitability	Use
Arthur's Rock	Natural	Foot	High
Audra Culver	Natural	Foot/bike/horse	Low
Besant Point	Natural	Foot / bike/horse	Low to moderate
Black Powder	Natural	Foot	Low to moderate
Carey Springs	Natural	Foot / bike/horse	Low
Coyote Ridge	Natural	Foot / bike/horse	Moderate
Devil's Backbone	Natural	Foot / bike/horse	Moderate
East Valley	Natural	Foot / bike/horse	Moderate
Fawn Hollow	Natural	Foot / bike/horse	Low
Foothills	Natural	Foot / bike/horse	Moderate
Fossil Creek	Paved	Foot / bike/horse	Moderate
Greyrock	Natural	Foot	High
Herrington	Natural	Foot / bike/horse	Low to moderate
Hewlett Gulch	Natural	Foot / bike/horse	Moderate to high
Horsetooth Falls	Natural	Foot / bike/horse	Moderate
Horsetooth Rock	Natural	Foot / bike/horse	High
Loggers	Natural	Foot / bike/horse	Low to moderate
Loveland Recreation	Paved	Foot / bike	Moderate
Mill Creek	Natural	Foot/bike/horse	Moderate
Mill Creek Link	Natural	Foot / bike/horse	Moderate
Nomad	Natural	Foot / bike/horse	Low
Overlook (Lory)	Natural	Foot	Moderate
Overlook (Gateway)	Natural	Foot	Low to moderate

Trail Summary Table cont'd

Trail	Length one way	Elevation	Difficulty
Pineridge trails	7.00 mi	5,140' - 5,475'	Easy
Pleasant Valley	1.40 mi	5,050' - 5,099'	Easy
Poudre River (Ft Col)	10.00 mi	4,871' - 5,009'	Easy
Poudre River (Windsor)	9.90 mi	4,697' - 4,777'	Easy
Power	1.73 mi	4,937' - 4,954'	Easy
Round Mountain	4.87 mi	5,794' - 8,449'	Moderate
Sawmill	1.15 mi	5,553' - 6,192'	Moderate
Shoreline	.70 mi	5,433' - 5,690'	Easy to moderate
Shoshone	1.50 mi	6,570' - 6,853'	Easy to moderate
Soderberg	1.38 mi	5,805' - 6,204'	Easy to moderate
South Valley	2.38 mi	5,462' - 5,645'	Easy
Spring Creek (Ft Col)	7.14 mi	4,894' - 5,128'	Easy
Spring Creek (HTMP)	2.17 mi	5,849' - 6,918'	Moderate
Stout	2.87 mi	5,874' - 6,479'	Easy to moderate
Sundance	3.13 mi	5,756' - 5,796'	Easy
Timber	3.55 mi	5,583' - 6,778'	Moderate
Waterfall	.04 mi	5,610' - 5,620'	Easy
Wathen	.96 mi	6,242' - 6,846'	Moderate
Well Gulch	1.34 mi	5,507' - 5,877'	Easy to moderate
West Valley	2.00 mi	5,506' - 5,683'	Easy
Westridge (HTMP)	1.71 mi	6,835' - 7,093'	Easy to moderate
Westridge (Lory)	1.52 mi	6,691' - 6,975'	Easy
Young Gulch	5.02 mi	5,813' - 6,998'	Easy

HTMP - Horsetooth Mountain Park
Lory   - Lory State Park

Trail	Surface	Suitability	Use
Pineridge trails	Natural	Foot / bike/horse	Moderate
Pleasant Valley	Paved	Foot / bikes	Low
Poudre River (Ft Col)	Paved	Foot / bike/horse	High
Poudre River (Windsor)	Paved	Foot / bike/horse	Moderate
Power	Paved	Foot / bike	Low
Round Mountain	Natural	Foot / bike/horse	Low to moderate
Sawmill	Natural	Foot / bike/horse	Low to moderate
Shoreline	Natural	Foot / bike/horse	Low to moderate
Shoshone	Natural	Foot / bike/horse	Low to moderate
Soderberg	Natural	Foot / bike/horse	Moderate
South Valley	Natural	Foot / bike/horse	Moderate
Spring Creek (Ft Col)	Paved	Foot/ bike	High
Spring Creek (HTMP)	Natural	Foot / bike/horse	Low to moderate
Stout	Natural	Foot / bike/horse	Low to moderate
Sundance	Natural	Foot / bike/horse	Low to moderate
Timber	Natural	Foot	Moderate
Waterfall	Natural	Foot	Moderate
Wathen	Natural	Foot / bike/horse	Moderate
Well Gulch	Natural	Foot	Moderate
West Valley	Natural	Foot / bike/horse	Moderate
Westridge (HTMP)	Natural	Foot / bike/horse	Low to moderate
Westridge (Lory)	Natural	Foot	Low
Young Gulch	Natural	Foot / bike/horse	Moderate

HTMP - Horsetooth Mountain Park
Lory   - Lory State Park

determined for hiking the trails from left to right on the altitude profiles. If you hike in the opposite directions they will be reversed.

Trails and trail sections are rated for difficulty. Rating trail difficulty is not easy as so much depends on the physical condition of the hiker. What is easy for one may be moderate or strenuous for someone else. I have tried to come up with some objective criteria for rating trail difficulty for a hiker in average physical condition. For me, the steepness of a trail, the roughness of the trail surface (how much stepping up or down), and the elevations that are traversed determine how difficult a trail or section of trail is. Although the length of a trail influences the total amount of energy expended in hiking it, not all trails are hiked in one day. It may be misleading to include trail length in difficulty rating criteria. Also, the rating of some trails may be heavily influenced by a small, strenuous section. Therefore, over 50 percent of a moderate to strenuous trail could be easy to hike. For these reasons I have selected slope (change in elevation divided by the distance traveled horizontally) as the primary criterion for trail difficulty. Although not scientifically tested, I chose slopes from 0 - 8 percent as easy, 9 - 25 percent as moderate, and slopes greater than 25 percent as strenuous. I subjectively included surface roughness and elevation where they were deemed to influence difficulty. Slopes were computed for .1 mile intervals along each trail. Bands of continuous difficulty ratings are color coded on the altitude profiles for each trail. Elevation gains and losses are the sum of the gains and losses for each of the .1 mile intervals. The change in elevation is the sum of the total gains and losses over the entire length of the trail.

Length (one way)	2.26 miles (3.64 kilometers)
Elevation change	204 feet
Difficulty	Easy
Season	All year (sunrise to sunset)
Suitability	Hiking, mountain biking, horseback riding
Usage	Low to moderate
Restrictions	Park permit required Pets must be on a leash
Nearest trailhead	Blue Mountain Trailhead Ramsay-Shockey Trailhead

The Besant Point Trail is located near Pinewood Lake. This 2.26 mile long trail is easy to hike. It can be accessed on the south from the Blue Mountain Trailhead and on the north from the Ramsay-Shockey Trailhead. A Larimer County Parks pass is required to use this trail. From the north, the trail crosses the

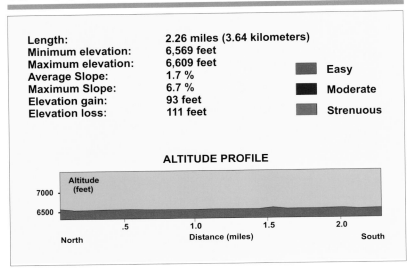

Length:	2.26 miles (3.64 kilometers)
Minimum elevation:	6,569 feet
Maximum elevation:	6,609 feet
Average Slope:	1.7 %
Maximum Slope:	6.7 %
Elevation gain:	93 feet
Elevation loss:	111 feet

Easy

Moderate

Strenuous

ALTITUDE PROFILE

spillway and dam and travels about .26 miles to its intersection with the north end of the Shoshone Trail. There is a restroom here. It continues around Fisherman's Cove, a long, narrow inlet to the lake, for about a half mile to its intersection with the south end of the Shoshone Trail. The trail makes a path along the western shore of Pinewood Lake, traveling close

The trail makes a winding path along the west shore of Pinewood Lake.

to the water as well as moving away from the shore in places. It primarily travels through open, grassy areas. There are walkways over a few wet areas near the south end of the trail. The trail crosses above an area of small cliffs where there is a sign warning you to stay off of the cliffs. The last three tenths of a mile of the southern end of the trail is wheelchair-

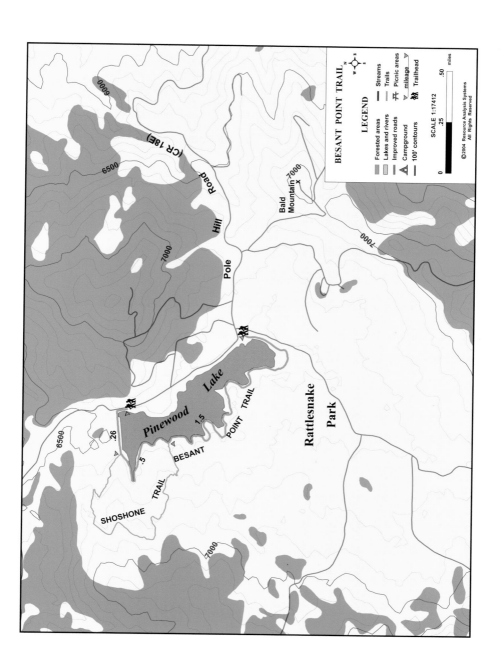

BESANT POINT TRAIL

LEGEND

Forested areas — Streams
Lakes and rivers — Trails
Improved roads — Picnic areas
△ Campground — ▼ mileage
100' contours — 🅇 Trailhead

SCALE 1:17412

0   .25   .50
miles

©2004 Resource Analysis Systems
All Rights Reserved

6000

(CR 18E)

6500

Hill Road

7000

Pole

Bald
Mountain
X 7000

7000

Pinewood Lake

POINT TRAIL

BESANT

Rattlesnake

Park

6500

.26

.5

1.5

SHOSHONE

TRAIL

7000

accessible including a gravel path and wooden boardwalk. Riders should dismount while on the boardwalk. The Besant Point Trail offers a pleasant walk with great views of the lake

Here the trail intersects with the south end of the Shoshone Trail.

and surrounding scenery as well as access to fishing.

Directons:

The Besant Point Trail is located near Pinewood Lake. Take Highway 34 west from Loveland to County Road 29. Turn south on CR 29 and travel about two miles to CR 18E. Turn west on CR18E and travel about 6.7 miles to Pinewood Lake. The trail begins on the south at the Blue Mountain Trailhead and on the north at the Ramsay-Shockey Trailhead. A fee is required to park at the trailheads.

Length (one way)	.63 miles (1.01 kilometers)
Elevation change	410 feet
Difficulty	Moderate
Season	All year (7am to 9pm in summer, 8am to sunset rest of year)
Suitability	Hiking
Usage	Low to moderate
Restrictions	Park permit required Pets must be on a leash
Nearest trailhead	Gateway Mountain Park

     The Black Powder Trail is a new trail that was built by Volunteers For Outdoor Colorado in September of 2003. It is located in Gateway Mountain Park. The trail is of moderate difficulty traveling about .63 miles from the Seaman Reservoir Road to a point above the Poudre Canyon. There is a short

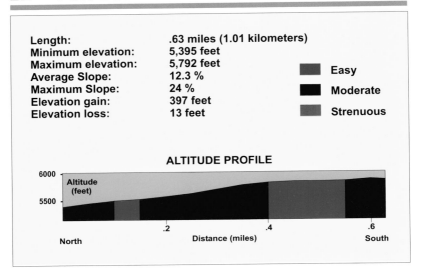

Length: .63 miles (1.01 kilometers)
Minimum elevation: 5,395 feet
Maximum elevation: 5,792 feet
Average Slope: 12.3 %   ▮ Easy
Maximum Slope: 24 %
Elevation gain: 397 feet   ▮ Moderate
Elevation loss: 13 feet
                                                 ▮ Strenuous

ALTITUDE PROFILE

(.08 miles) spur trail connected to it that offers additional views. The Black Powder Trail travels through a ponderosa

pine forest as it climbs the ridge east of the river. It makes several switchbacks along the way. Once on top of the ridge, it travels through an open, grassy area to a knoll above Poudre Canyon. The trail begins at an elevation of 5,395 feet

The trail climbs through an open area as it approaches the knoll above Poudre Canyon.

and climbs to 5,778 feet on the knoll. You get great views of Gateway Mountain Park, Seaman Reservoir, and Poudre Canyon from the trail. Although rated moderate in difficulty, sections of the trail border on being in the strenuous category. It takes about 1 to 1.5 hours to hike.

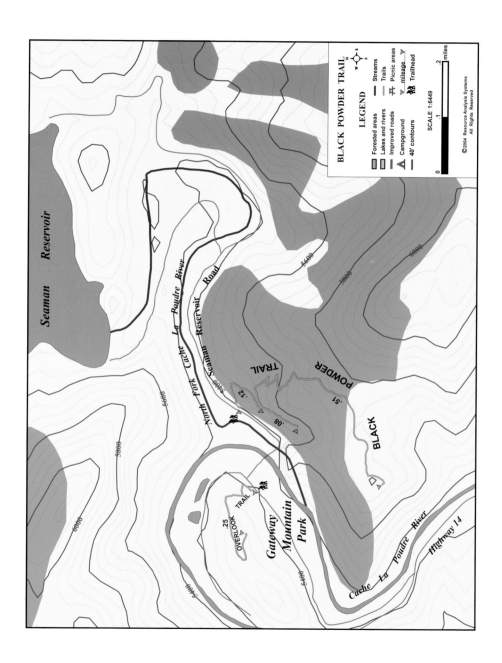

BLACK POWDER TRAIL

LEGEND

Forested areas
Lakes and rivers
Improved roads
Campground
40' contours

Streams
Trails
Picnic areas
mileage
Trailhead

SCALE 1:6449

©2004 Resource Analysis Systems
All Rights Reserved

Seaman Reservoir

Cache La Poudre River

North Fork Seaman Reservoir Road

POWDER TRAIL

BLACK

Gateway Mountain Park

OVERLOOK TRAIL

.25

.12

.80

.51

Cache La Poudre River

Highway 14

Another small trail (Overlook Trail) is located in Gateway Mountain Park. This short (.25 miles) trail offers great views of the park and areas of planned development.

You get a great view of Poudre Canyon from the end of the trail.

The Overlook Trail is easy to hike.

Directions:

The Black Powder Trail is located in Poudre Canyon. Take Highway 287 north from Fort Collins to Laporte. Continue on 287 to Highway 14. Travel west on 14 for about 5.2 miles to Gateway Mountain Park. The trail begins from the Seaman Reservoir Road about .15 miles from the north end of the park.

Length (one way)	3.71 miles (5.98 kilometers)
Elevation change	1,115 feet
Difficulty	Easy to moderate
Season	All year (5am to 11pm)
Suitability	Hiking, mountain biking, horseback riding
Usage	Moderate
Restrictions	Pets are not permitted
Nearest trailhead	Coyote Ridge Trailhead

The Coyote Ridge Trail is a great hiking, biking, and horseback riding trail that travels through the Coyote Ridge Natural Area and Rimrock Open Space Area. It makes a 3.7 mile path over two hogbacks and across a beautiful valley in between. The trail follows a roadway west for the first .7 miles. It reaches a cabin and building at the end of the road. There is

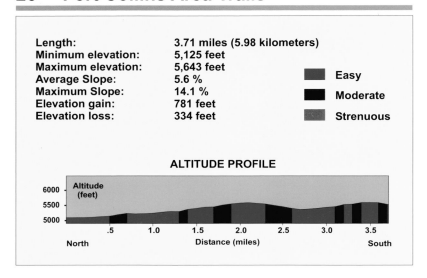

Length:	3.71 miles (5.98 kilometers)
Minimum elevation:	5,125 feet
Maximum elevation:	5,643 feet
Average Slope:	5.6 %
Maximum Slope:	14.1 %
Elevation gain:	781 feet
Elevation loss:	334 feet

■ Easy
■ Moderate
■ Strenuous

ALTITUDE PROFILE

Altitude (feet)

6000
5500
5000

.5   1.0   1.5   2.0   2.5   3.0   3.5

North   Distance (miles)   South

a vault toilet and telephone near the building. From here the trail becomes more narrow and turns north along the ridge.

After traveling a short distance it travels through a gap in the ridge, crosses a small valley, and climbs the first hogback. The view is quite striking as you climb the hogback. Well worth the effort. Once you reach the top, the trail levels out and enters

The trail climbs the first hogback after passing through a gap in the first ridge.

the Rimrock Open Space. Here you get magnificent views to the east and west. It follows the ridgeline and then descends to the west into a small valley. The trail travels over a series of steps where it is recommended that bikers and horsemen dismount while climbing down over them.

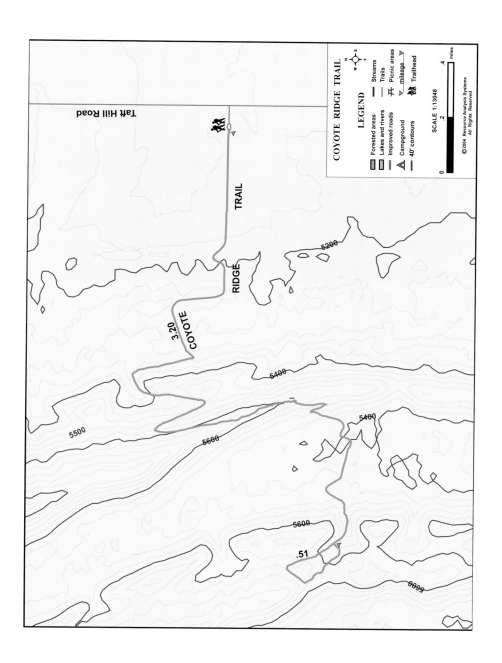

COYOTE RIDGE TRAIL

LEGEND

Forested areas
Lakes and rivers
Improved roads
△ Campground
40' contours

— Streams
— Trails
⊤ Picnic areas
▽ mileage
🚶 Trailhead

N
W — E
S

SCALE 1:13048

0   .2   .4
miles

©2004 Resource Analysis Systems
All Rights Reserved

Taft Hill Road

TRAIL

RIDGE

COYOTE

3.20

5200

5400

5400

5500

5600

5600

6000

.51

After crossing the valley, the trail passes through a fence and heads up a gap in the second hogback. It contours

The trail travels across this beautiful valley between the hogbacks.

along the north side of the gap as it climbs toward the top of the ridge. The trail soon comes to an intersection where it makes a half mile loop through the red rocks. About 70% of the trail is easy to hike with the rest being of moderate difficulty. It takes about three hours to make the 6.9 mile round trip.

Directions:

The Coyote Ridge Trail is located between Fort Collins and Loveland. Take Taft Hill Road for about one mile south of Trilby Road to the parking area west of the highway.

Length (one way)	3.56 miles (5.73 kilometers)
Elevation change	1,021 feet
Difficulty	Easy to moderate
Season	All year (sunrise to sunset)
Suitability	Hiking, mountain biking, horseback riding
Usage	Moderate
Restrictions	Pets must be on a leash Rock climbing is prohibited
Nearest trailhead	Devil's Backbone Trailhead

The Devil's Backbone Trail offers an easy to moderate hike along the strikingly beautiful rock formation known as the Devil's Backbone. This trail is located in the Devil's Backbone Open Space just west of Loveland. The trail begins at an elevation of 5,069 feet and travels about 3.5 miles north to an elevation of 5,479 feet at the end of a loop. The total elevation gain is 717 feet. This is a good trail for hiking, mountain

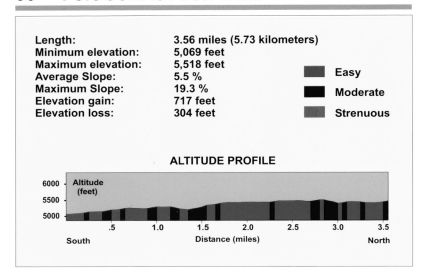

Length: 3.56 miles (5.73 kilometers)
Minimum elevation: 5,069 feet
Maximum elevation: 5,518 feet
Average Slope: 5.5 %
Maximum Slope: 19.3 %
Elevation gain: 717 feet
Elevation loss: 304 feet

Easy
Moderate
Strenuous

ALTITUDE PROFILE

biking, running, horseback riding, or wildlife viewing. Several species of raptors including red-tailed hawks, golden eagles,

You get a great view of the Devil's Backbone from the ridge to the east.

and great horned owls live in the area. Ravens also occupy the area. Rattlesnakes have been seen on and around the trail during warmer months.

The trail begins at the trailhead just off Highway 34 and travels north along the east side of the Devil's Backbone. It soon splits into foot only and multi-purpose trails. The foot only trail travels much closer to the rock formations. There are interpretive posts along the foot trail as well as benches for rest stops. The foot trail leads to the Keyhole, a large hole in the rocks where you can see a long distance both east and west. The views from

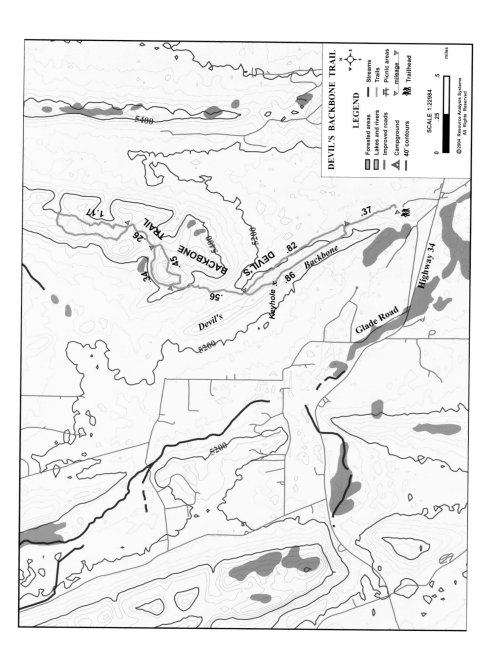

DEVIL'S BACKBONE TRAIL

LEGEND

- Forested areas
- Lakes and rivers
- Improved roads
- ▲ Campground
- 40' contours
- Streams
- Trails
- ⛙ Picnic areas
- ▽ mileage
- 🚶 Trailhead

SCALE 1:22984

0   .25   .5

miles

©2004 Resource Analysis Systems
All Rights Reserved

the Keyhole are spectacular. There is a bench here for resting while taking in the view.

The Keyhole frames a beautiful view to the west.

From the Keyhole, the trail drops back down into the valley where it meets the multi-purpose trail. The trail crosses the valley and climbs the ridge to the east. This is the most strenuous part of the trail. You get great views of the Devil's Backbone as you near the top of the ridge. Here the trail splits, traveling around a knoll in both directions and rejoining on the opposite side. It continues across a flat, open area before beginning a 1.2 mile loop. This is a great hike or ride. Pets must be on a leash and rock climbing is prohibited.

Directions:

The Devil's Backbone Trail is located west of Loveland. Take Highway 34 west to the trailhead just north of the highway. It is located about a half mile east of Glade Road. There is a water tank near the highway at the top of a rise where you turn off to the parking area.

Length (one way)	.73 miles (1.17 kilometers)
Elevation change	294 feet
Difficulty	Easy to moderate
Season	All year
Suitability	Hiking, mountain biking, horseback riding
Usage	Low
Restrictions	Park permit required Pets must be on a leash
Nearest trailhead	Saddle Trailhead

   The Fawn Hollow Trail is located near Carter Lake in the foothills west of Loveland. This trail is about .73 miles long and travels across the ridge to the east of Carter Lake. You can access the trail on the north near Dam 1 and on the south from the Saddle Parking Area. Parking is limited near the dam.

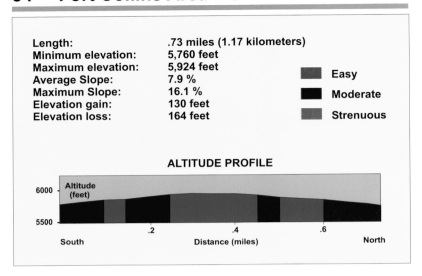

Length:	.73 miles (1.17 kilometers)
Minimum elevation:	5,760 feet
Maximum elevation:	5,924 feet
Average Slope:	7.9 %
Maximum Slope:	16.1 %
Elevation gain:	130 feet
Elevation loss:	164 feet

Easy

Moderate

Strenuous

ALTITUDE PROFILE

Altitude (feet)

6000

5500

.2   .4   .6

South   Distance (miles)   North

The trail is easy to moderate in difficulty (50/50). It leaves the west end of the Saddle Parking Area and soon makes an

abrupt right turn away from the lake. The other trail that travels parallel to the lake shore (straight ahead) provides access for rock climbers. The Fawn Hollow Trail makes a moderate climb up the ridge over a rocky surface. Once on top, the trail

The trail travels through this grassy area on its way toward Dam 1.

is fairly easy going. This trail can be faint in spots but just keep going in its general direction and you'll pick it up again. There is a lot of deer sign along the trail so keep a look out for mule deer during early and late hours. You get great views of the lake and the mountains to the west where the trail travels along the top of the ridge. After a short distance along the

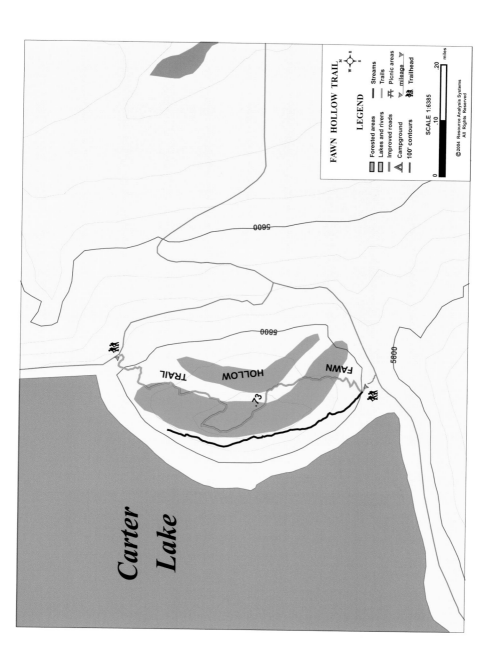

Carter Lake

FAWN HOLLOW TRAIL

LEGEND

Forested areas
Lakes and rivers
Improved roads
Campground
100' contours

Streams
Trails
Picnic areas
mileage
Trailhead

SCALE 1:6385

0   .10   .20
                    miles

©2004 Resource Analysis Systems
All Rights Reserved

FAWN HOLLOW TRAIL

5600

5600

5600

.73

You get a great view of Carter Lake and the mountains to the west where the trail follows the top of the ridge.

ridgeline, the trail makes a serpentine path to its north end near Dam 1. A Larimer County Parks Pass is required to use this trail.

Directions:

The Fawn Hollow Trail is located near Carter Lake. Take Highway 34 west from Loveland to County Road 29. Turn south on CR 29 and travel about two miles to CR 18E. Turn west on CR18E and go about 2.2 miles to the entrance to Carter Lake. A fee is required to park at the trailhead. Follow the road around to the south end of the lake. The Saddle Parking Area is about a mile past Dam 1. The south end of the trail is at the west end of the parking area.

Length (one way)	6.07 miles (9.77 kilometers)
Elevation change	2,193 feet
Difficulty	Easy to moderate
Season	All year
Suitability	Hiking, mountain biking, horseback riding
Usage	Moderate
Restrictions	Pets must be on a leash
Nearest trailhead	Michaud Lane Centennial Drive

The Foothills Trail is an unpaved trail that travels up and down the foothills west of Fort Collins in a north-south direction. It both loses and gains over 1,000 feet over its 6.1 mile length. The trail begins at the west end of Michaud Lane. It makes a straight path to the west, traveling between two fence lines across private property. It intersects a trail to the

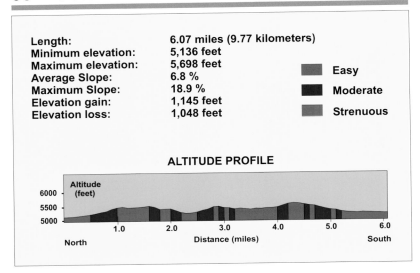

Length:	6.07 miles (9.77 kilometers)
Minimum elevation:	5,136 feet
Maximum elevation:	5,698 feet
Average Slope:	6.8 %
Maximum Slope:	18.9 %
Elevation gain:	1,145 feet
Elevation loss:	1,048 feet

Easy

Moderate

Strenuous

ALTITUDE PROFILE

Altitude (feet)

North   Distance (miles)   South

Centennial Drive Parking Area soon after it begins to climb the foothills. This trail to the right loops north and then south for about a mile before ending at Centennial Drive. You get a good view of the Bellvue Valley as well as Horsetooth Reservoir and its North Dam from this loop trail.

About a mile of the trail travels along the shore of Horsetooth Reservoir.

The Foothills Trail continues south from the loop trail intersection and intersects a shorter trail leading to Centennial Drive. You get great views of Fort Collins from sections of the Foothills Trail traveling along the east side of the ridge. Although rocky, over 65% of the trail is easy to hike. A few sections of the trail come close to Centennial Drive. The trail is closed near the Soldier Canyon and Dixon dams as they

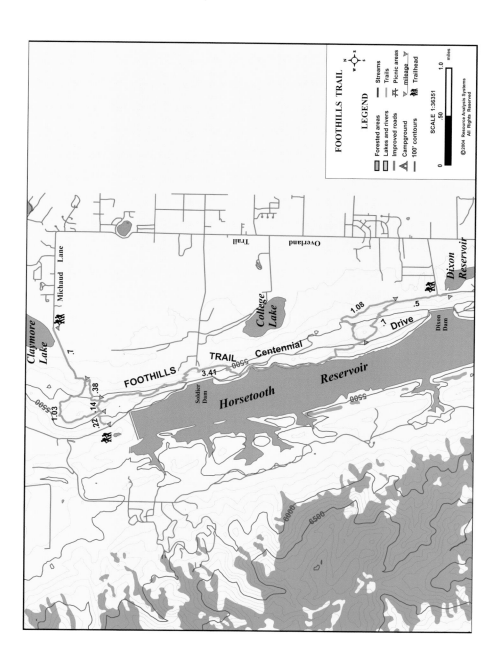

FOOTHILLS TRAIL

LEGEND

Forested areas		Streams	
Lakes and rivers		Trails	
Improved roads		Picnic areas	
Campground		mileage	
100' contours		Trailhead	

SCALE 1:36351

0   .50   1.0
miles

©2004 Resource Analysis Systems
All Rights Reserved

Claymore Lake

Michaud Lane

Overland Trail

College Lake

Dixon Reservoir

FOOTHILLS   TRAIL   Centennial   Drive

Soldier Dam

Horsetooth   Reservoir

Dixon Dam

5500

5500

6500

6900

.7

1.03
.22 .14 .38

3.41

1.08

.7

.5

finish work on them. Take a short spur trail to Centennial Drive just before the trail descends toward Soldier Dam to get around it. Access the trail near Hughes Stadium to get around Dixon Dam. From the south side of Soldier Dam, the trail

After crossing Centennial Drive, the trail makes its way down the ridge to the east behind Hughes Stadium.

climbs the ridge and crosses Centennial Drive. It then drops down to Horsetooth Reservoir and travels along the shoreline in a southerly direction. After traveling a little over a mile, the trail climbs the ridge and crosses over Centennial Drive to the east. From here it descends the ridge behind Hughes Stadium. The trail continues south past Dixon Dam (currently closed) to Dixon Reservoir.

Directons:

The Foothills Trail can be accessed from Michaud Lane, Centennial Drive, or Hughes Stadium. Michaud Lane is located on Overland Trail where the road makes an "S" shaped curve. The trail begins at the west end of Michaud Lane.

Length (one way)	2.39 miles (3.84 kilometers)
Elevation change	206 feet
Difficulty	Easy
Season	All year
Suitability	Hiking, mountain biking, roller blading, horseback riding
Usage	Moderate
Restrictions	Pets must be on a leash Horses must stay within 10 feet of path
Nearest trailhead	Shields Trailhead Harmony Trailhead

The Fossil Creek Trail is located in the Cathy Fromme Prairie Natural Area. This paved trail travels west from Shields Street to a point north and west of Taft Hill Road. There are three access points to this trail: a trailhead on South Shields just south of Front Range Community College, a trailhead at

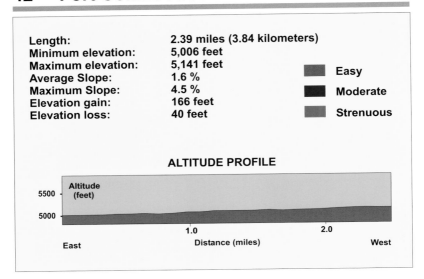

Length:	2.39 miles (3.84 kilometers)
Minimum elevation:	5,006 feet
Maximum elevation:	5,141 feet
Average Slope:	1.6 %
Maximum Slope:	4.5 %
Elevation gain:	166 feet
Elevation loss:	40 feet

Easy

Moderate

Strenuous

ALTITUDE PROFILE

Altitude (feet)

5500

5000

1.0   2.0

East   Distance (miles)   West

the west end of old Harmony Road, and the west end of the trail near West Ridge Estates. Although primarily used by hikers

The trail passes under Taft Hill Road near the trailhead on old Harmony Road.

and bicyclists, horses are permitted on the trail. However, they must stay within 10 feet of the paved pathway. There is not much room for horse trailers at the Shields parking area but ample room at the Harmony parking area.

This trail travels through short grass prairie, giving you a feeling for what it was like before the town was settled. There are numerous opportunities for viewing wildlife including birds, raptors, prairie dogs, rabbits, deer, and rattlesnakes. A memorial to Cathy Fromme is located near the east end of the trail. The trail travels northwest through the prairie and past

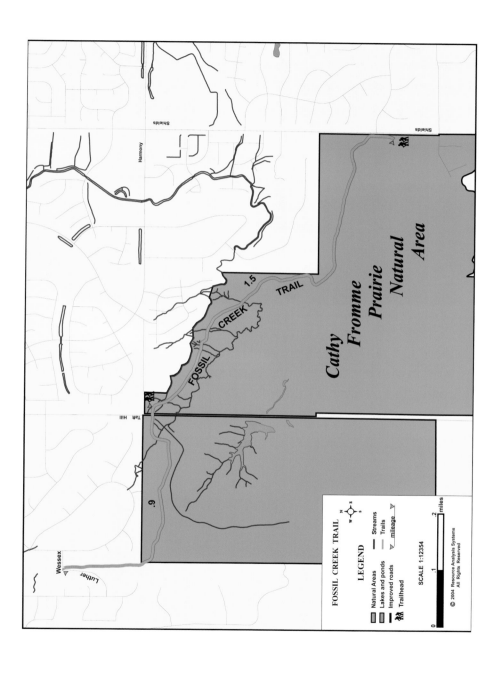

Cathy Fromme Prairie Natural Area

Shields

Harmony

Shields

FOSSIL CREEK TRAIL

1.5

FOSSIL CREEK TRAIL

1¼

Taft Hill

.9

Wessex

Luther

LEGEND

Natural Areas
Lakes and ponds
Improved roads
Trailhead

Streams
Trails
mileage

SCALE 1:12354

0   .1   .2   miles

© 2004 Resource Analysis Systems
All Rights Reserved

wetlands where red-winged blackbirds stake out their territories and sing their songs. It makes a gradual climb, gaining about 166 feet in elevation over its 2.4 mile length. After crossing

The Cathy Fromme Prairie shows you what it was like before the town of Fort Collins was built.

under Taft Hill Road, the trail continues west and then turns north just east of West Ridge Estates. It soon ends at a road leading to West Ridge Estates.

Directions:

The Fossil Creek Trail is located in the city of Fort Collins. Its primary access point is from South Shields about .6 miles south of Harmony Road. There is also a large parking area at the west end of old Harmony Road.

Greyrock

Length (one way)	Meadow - 4.46 mi (7.18 km) Summit - 3.16 mi (5.09 km)
Elevation change	Meadow - 2,679 feet Summit - 1,991 feet
Difficulty	Moderate
Season	All year
Suitability	Hiking
Usage	High
Restrictions	Pets must be on a leash
Nearest trailhead	Greyrock Trailhead

Greyrock Trail is 19.4 miles from Fort Collins. The parking area is on the left side of the road and will hold about two dozen vehicles. The parking area is for day use only with the exception of backpackers. The trail starts on the other side of the Poudre River across a wooden foot bridge. It climbs gently west for about .6 miles to a junction where it splits into the Meadow and Summit trails. The trails take different routes and rejoin near the summit of Greyrock Mountain. You can

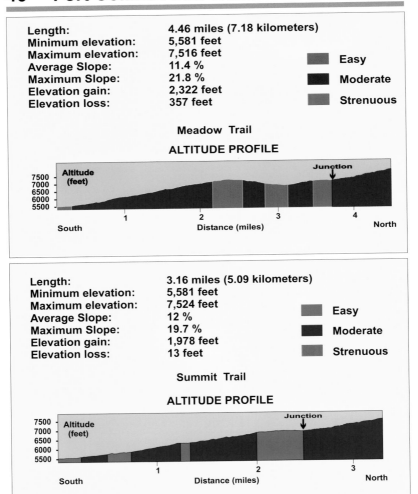

Length:	4.46 miles (7.18 kilometers)
Minimum elevation:	5,581 feet
Maximum elevation:	7,516 feet
Average Slope:	11.4 %
Maximum Slope:	21.8 %
Elevation gain:	2,322 feet
Elevation loss:	357 feet

Easy

Moderate

Strenuous

Meadow Trail

ALTITUDE PROFILE

Length:	3.16 miles (5.09 kilometers)
Minimum elevation:	5,581 feet
Maximum elevation:	7,524 feet
Average Slope:	12 %
Maximum Slope:	19.7 %
Elevation gain:	1,978 feet
Elevation loss:	13 feet

Easy

Moderate

Strenuous

Summit Trail

ALTITUDE PROFILE

make a loop by taking one trail up and the other trail back.

It is about .9 miles from the junction to the summit of Greyrock Mountain. About two thirds of the trail to the summit is moderate to strenuous. It climbs over and around large rocks and at times is difficult to find. Rock cairns mark the way in some spots. At the top there is a small pond occupied by frogs. The view here is spectacular.

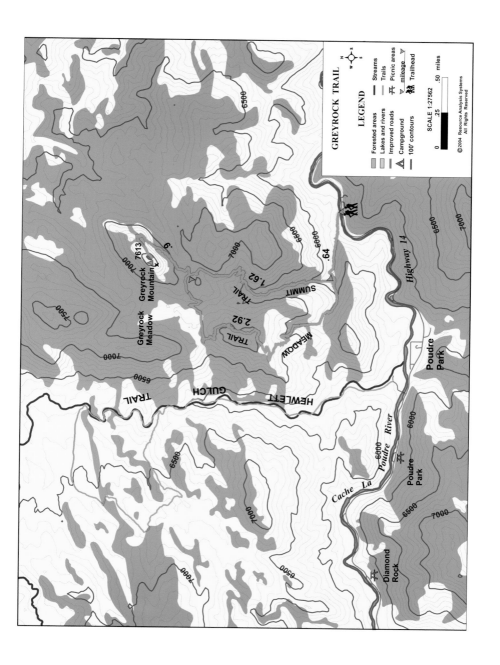

GREYROCK TRAIL

LEGEND

- Forested areas
- Lakes and rivers
- Improved roads
- ▲ Campground
- 100' contours
- — Streams
- — Trails
- 开 Picnic areas
- ▽ mileage
- 🛉 Trailhead

SCALE 1:27562

0   .25   .50 miles

©2004 Resource Analysis Systems
All Rights Reserved

Greyrock Mountain 7613

6'

Greyrock Meadow

SUMMIT TRAIL

1.62

2.92

MEADOW TRAIL

.64

HEWLETT GULCH TRAIL

Highway 14

Poudre Park

Cache La Poudre River

Poudre Park

Diamond Rock

The total length of the loop (Meadow and Summit trails without going to the top) is about 5.7 miles. The trails are of moderate difficulty. Gorgeous views can be seen at many points along the way.

You get a great view from the summit of Greyrock Mountain.

Directions:

The Greyrock Trail is located in Poudre Canyon. Take Highway 287 north from Fort Collins to Laporte. Continue on 287 to Highway 14. Travel west on 14 for seven miles to the trailhead. The parking lot is on the left side of the highway. The trail begins on the north side of the Poudre River. There is a bridge below the right side of the highway.

Length (one way)	5.7 miles (9.17 kilometers)
Elevation change	2,017 feet
Difficulty	Easy to moderate
Season	All year
Suitability	Hiking, mountain biking, horseback riding
Usage	Moderate to high
Restrictions	Pets must be on a leash
Nearest trailhead	Just west of Poudre Park

The Hewlett Gulch Trail is a popular mountain bike trail located near Pourde Park. This trail is also good for hiking or horseback riding. The trail begins a short distance north of the Poudre River and travels north along a small stream for a little over two miles. It then makes a 3.7 mile loop that comes back to the main trail. The total length for a round trip is about eight miles. About 73% of the trail is easy to hike with the rest

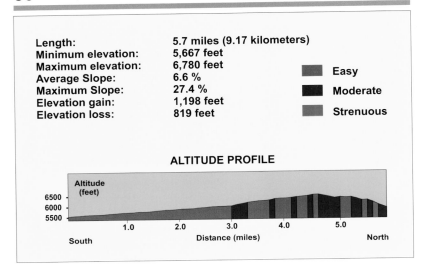

Length:	5.7 miles (9.17 kilometers)
Minimum elevation:	5,667 feet
Maximum elevation:	6,780 feet
Average Slope:	6.6 %
Maximum Slope:	27.4 %
Elevation gain:	1,198 feet
Elevation loss:	819 feet

■ Easy

■ Moderate

■ Strenuous

ALTITUDE PROFILE

being moderate with a short section that is strenuous.

The first 2.1 miles of the trail makes numerous crossings of a small stream. The stream is shallow and easy to cross. The trail is generally smooth and easy walking, although stream crossings are fairly rocky. It travels through a number of

The trail crosses a large meadow at the top of the loop section.

large meadows with clumps of trees near the stream. You get great views of the surrounding foothills. Look for mule deer grazing on the hillsides. The trail passes through an area that was burned in a recent fire. The grass and weeds can be quite high following a wet spring. At the end of this first stretch it begins a 3.7 mile circular loop, returning to its starting point.

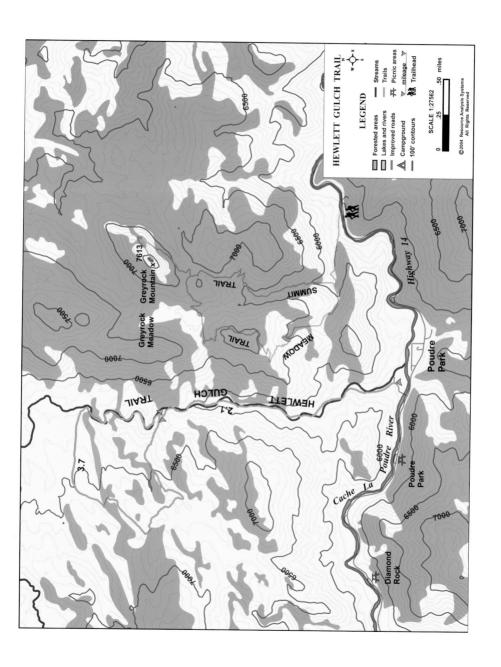

HEWLETT GULCH TRAIL

LEGEND

Forested areas
Lakes and rivers
Improved roads
100' contours

Streams
Trails
Picnic areas
Campground
mileage
Trailhead

SCALE 1:27562

0   .25   .50   miles

©2004 Resource Analysis Systems
All Rights Reserved

The trail climbs out of the gulch and across the open ridge to the west before descending (steep and rough in spots) back down into Hewlett Gulch and meeting the first trail section

The trail gets a little gnarly here for mountain bikers.

again. At one point the trail comes to a "T" intersection. Turn left to return to the main trail. There is one section that is steep and very rocky. Mountain bikers should be careful here.

Directions:

The Hewlett Gulch Trail is located in Poudre Canyon. Take Highway 287 north from Fort Collins to Laporte. Continue on 287 to Highway 14. Travel west on 14 for about eleven miles to Poudre Park. The trail is about a half mile west of Poudre Park. There is a bridge crossing the Poudre River. This is a private road so park along Highway 14 and walk or ride over the bridge. The trail begins a short distance north of the river from a dirt road.

Horsetooth Mountain Park is located south of Lory State Park and west of Horsetooth Reservoir, about four miles from Fort Collins. It is named for the very familiar landmark, Horsetooth Rock. The park contains over 2,300 acres of open, grassy meadowlands and ponderosa pine/ douglas fir forest. There are about twenty miles of trails in the park ranging from easy to moderate in difficulty. All of the trails are open to foot, mountain bike, and horseback use. Elevations range from 5,430 feet at Horsetooth Reservoir to 7,255 feet at the top of Horsetooth Rock. The park is open year round for your enjoyment. This is a great area for wildflowers, wildlife, and scenic vistas. Trails here offer spectacular views of Horsetooth Reservoir, Fort Collins, and the plains to the east. Climbing Horsetooth Rock is very popular. The trails leading to the rock can be very busy during the warmer months of the year.

A daily entrance permit or annual pass is required to use the park. Self pay stations are available at the park entrance.

Horsetooth Mountain Park Trails

TRAIL	LENGTH (one way)	DIFFICULTY	SUITABILITY
Audra Culver	.67 miles	Moderate	Foot, bicycle, horseback
Carey Springs	.24 miles	Easy	Foot, bicycle, horseback
Herrington	.80 miles	Moderate	Foot, bicycle, horseback
Horsetooth Falls	.82 miles	Easy to moderate	Foot, bicycle, horseback
Horsetooth Rock	1.25 miles	Moderate	Foot, bicycle, horseback
Loggers	1.28 miles	Easy to moderate	Foot, bicycle, horseback
Mill Creek	2.91 miles	Moderate	Foot, bicycle, horseback
Nomad	1.04 miles	Easy	Foot, bicycle, horseback
Sawmill	1.15 miles	Moderate	Foot, bicycle, horseback
Soderberg	1.38 miles	Easy to moderate	Foot, bicycle, horseback
Spring Creek	2.17 miles	Moderate	Foot, bicycle, horseback
Stout	2.87 miles	Easy to moderate	Foot, bicycle, horseback
Wathen	.96 miles	Moderate	Foot, bicycle, horseback
Westridge	1.71 miles	Easy to moderate	Foot, bicycle, horseback

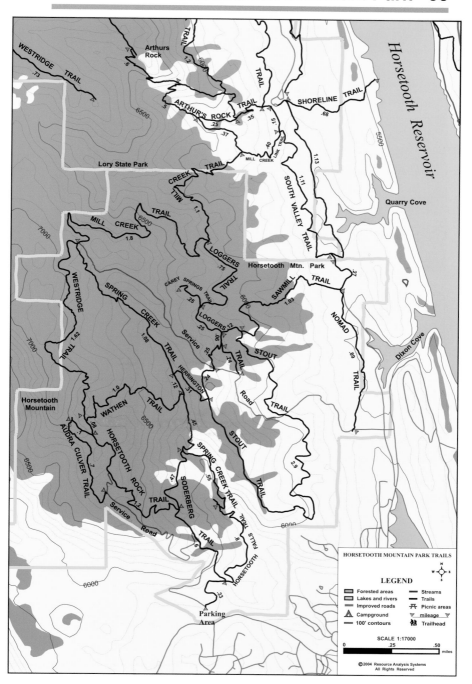

Horsetooth Reservoir

Arthurs Rock

WESTRIDGE TRAIL
.73
.6
.2
6500

TRAIL
6000

ARTHUR'S ROCK TRAIL
.5
.25
.37
.35
.15
.40
MILL CREEK
LINK TRAIL

SHORELINE TRAIL
.68

Quarry Cove

Lory State Park

MILL CREEK TRAIL
1.1

MILL CREEK TRAIL
1.8
6500
7000

SOUTH VALLEY TRAIL
1.11
1.13

Horsetooth Mtn. Park

LOGGERS TRAIL
.75

CAREY SPRINGS TRAIL
.25

SAWMILL TRAIL
1.03

NOMAD TRAIL
.89

.27

Dixon Cove

WESTRIDGE TRAIL 1.62

SPRING CREEK TRAIL
1.08

LOGGERS .12
.25
Service
.96
.23
.24

STOUT
.24

7000

Horsetooth Mountain

WATHEN TRAIL
1.0
.08
.7

HERRINGTON TRAIL
.12
.31
6500

Road

STOUT TRAIL
2.9

AUDRA CULVER TRAIL
.7

HORSETOOTH ROCK TRAIL
.42
1.2

SODERBERG TRAIL
.42
.55
.45

SPRING CREEK TRAIL
FALLS TRAIL
.8
.6

Service Road

6000

HORSETOOTH TRAIL
.33

Parking Area

6000

LEGEND

HORSETOOTH MOUNTAIN PARK TRAILS

Forested areas	Streams
Lakes and rivers	Trails
Improved roads	Picnic areas
Campground	mileage
100' contours	Trailhead

SCALE 1:17000

0   .25   .50
miles

Length (one way)	.67 miles (1.08 kilometers)
Elevation change	313 feet
Difficulty	Moderate
Season	All year
Suitability	Hiking, mountain biking, horseback riding
Usage	Low
Restrictions	Park permit required Pets must be on a leash
Nearest trailhead	Park entrance

The Audra Culver Trail is a relatively new trail in Horsetooth Mountain Park. This trail travels from the service road at 6,680 feet to just below Horsetooth Rock at 6,975 feet. The trail passes along the west facing slopes. This .7 mile long trail gives you great views of the Masonville Valley to the west. It passes through scattered ponderosa pines as it climbs toward

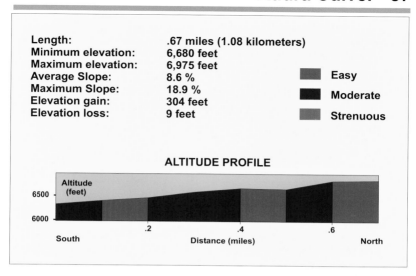

Length: .67 miles (1.08 kilometers)
Minimum elevation: 6,680 feet
Maximum elevation: 6,975 feet
Average Slope: 8.6 %   Easy
Maximum Slope: 18.9 %   Moderate
Elevation gain: 304 feet
Elevation loss: 9 feet   Strenuous

ALTITUDE PROFILE

Horsetooth Rock. Gaining 304 feet in elevation, sixty percent of this trail is of moderate difficulty with the rest being easy. Take the service road for 1.75 miles from the park entrance to reach this trail. The Audra Culver Trail is a good alternative route to or from Horsetooth Rock.

You get a great view of the Masonville Valley from the Audra Culver Trail.

The trail winds its way through stands of ponderosa pines.

Directions:

The Audra Culver Trail is located in Horsetooth Mountain Park. Take Harmony Road west until it reaches Taft Hill Road. Here Harmony Road becomes County Road 38E, continue straight. Follow County Road 38E around the south end of Horsetooth Reservoir, and at the top of the second hill, watch for the park entrance on the right. Take the service road for 1.75 miles from the park entrance to reach this trail.

Length (one way)	.24 miles (.38 kilometers)
Elevation change	67 feet
Difficulty	Easy
Season	All year
Suitability	Hiking, mountain biking, horseback riding
Usage	Low
Restrictions	Park permit required Pets must be on a leash
Nearest trailhead	Park entrance

The Carey Springs Trail is located in Horsetooth Mountain Park. This is a short trail that leads to Carey Springs and an old stock tank. The trail leaves the Loggers Trail and makes a gentle climb to the north and then southwest. This trail is only a quarter mile long and ends at a stock tank. This

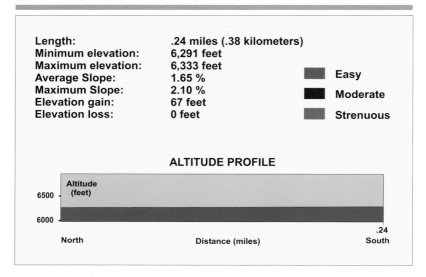

Length:	.24 miles (.38 kilometers)
Minimum elevation:	6,291 feet
Maximum elevation:	6,333 feet
Average Slope:	1.65 %
Maximum Slope:	2.10 %
Elevation gain:	67 feet
Elevation loss:	0 feet

Easy

Moderate

Strenuous

ALTITUDE PROFILE

Altitude (feet)

6500

6000

.24

North   Distance (miles)   South

tank used to contain water for watering horses and wildlife but is now empty. This trail is easy to hike as it gains only 67 feet in a quarter mile.

Directions:

The Carey Springs Trail is located in Horsetooth Mountain Park. Take Harmony Road west until it reaches Taft Hill Road. Here Harmony Road becomes County Road 38E, continue straight. Follow County Road 38E around the south end of Horsetooth Reservoir, and at the top of the second hill, watch for the park entrance on the right. Take the Soderberg Trail for about 1.4 miles to the Spring Creek Trail. Continue north for .55 miles to the Herrington Trail. Follow the Herrington Trail for .8 miles to the Loggers Trail. Continue north for .3 miles to the Carey Springs Trail.

Length (one way)	.8 miles (1.29 kilometers)
Elevation change	465 feet
Difficulty	Moderate
Season	All year
Suitability	Hiking, mountain biking, horseback riding
Usage	Low to moderate
Restrictions	Park permit required Pets must be on a leash
Nearest trailhead	Park entrance

The Herrington Trail is located in Horsetooth Mountain Park, connecting the Spring Creek Trail to the Stout and Loggers trails. It leaves the Spring Creek Trail and travels southeast, climbing the ridge to the east. You get a good view of Horsetooth Rock as you make the moderate climb. Black

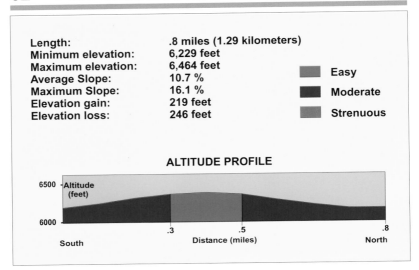

Length: .8 miles (1.29 kilometers)
Minimum elevation: 6,229 feet
Maximum elevation: 6,464 feet
Average Slope: 10.7 %   ▢ Easy
Maximum Slope: 16.1 %   ▢ Moderate
Elevation gain: 219 feet
Elevation loss: 246 feet   ▢ Strenuous

ALTITUDE PROFILE

bears have been occasionally seen in this area. The trail turns north at its intersection with the Stout Trail. It continues its climb, passing below some large rocks before descending to the service road. You must travel east on the service road for about one eighth of a mile to where the trail continues north.

The Herrington Trail leaves the Spring Creek Trail in a stand of ponderosa pines.

You get a great view of Horsetooth Rock from the Herrington Trail.

From here the trails winds its way down through ponderosa pines to the Loggers Trail. Climbing over a ridge, this trail gains and loses over 200 feet in elevation. About 75% of this short trail is of moderate difficulty.

Directions:

The Herrington Trail is located in Horsetooth Mountain Park. Take Harmony Road west until it reaches Taft Hill Road. Here Harmony Road becomes County Road 38E, continue straight. Follow County Road 38E around the south end of Horsetooth Reservoir, and at the top of the second hill, watch for the park entrance on the right. Take the Soderberg Trail for about 1.4 miles to the Spring Creek Trail. Continue north for .55 miles to the Herrington Trail.

Horsetooth Falls

Length (one way)	.82 miles (1.32 kilometers)
Elevation change	306 feet
Difficulty	Easy to moderate
Season	All year
Suitability	Hiking, mountain biking, horseback riding
Usage	Moderate
Restrictions	Park permit required Pets must be on a leash
Nearest trailhead	Park entrance

The Horsetooth Falls Trail is a relatively easy trail to hike with a few stretches of moderate difficulty. This trail is located in Horsetooth Mountain Park and makes a .8 mile path to Horsetooth Falls. Hiking this trail is a pleasant experience with great views and a relaxing respite at the base of the falls. The amount of water flowing over the falls is highly variable, with most water in the spring and very little in the fall and

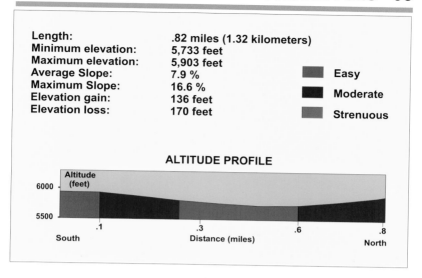

Length: .82 miles (1.32 kilometers)
Minimum elevation: 5,733 feet
Maximum elevation: 5,903 feet
Average Slope: 7.9 %
Maximum Slope: 16.6 %
Elevation gain: 136 feet
Elevation loss: 170 feet

■ Easy
■ Moderate
■ Strenuous

ALTITUDE PROFILE

winter. The trail begins from the Soderberg Trail at about 5,900 feet following a short hike of about .3 miles. It leads off to the east and then begins a descent along the ridge face to the northwest toward the valley containing the falls. There are benches and interpretive markers along the trail. The trail enters a narrow valley and crosses a creek over a wooden bridge. From here it

Here the trail crosses a creek over a small bridge.

climbs along the north side of the valley over some steps to its intersection with the Spring Creek Trail. It is a short descent to the base of the falls. There is a bench at the end of the trail to relax and enjoy the falls. This trail offers a pleasant walk through the foothills of northern Colorado.

The Horsetooth Falls Trail travels across the open hillside towards the gulch containing the falls.

Directions:

The Horsetooth Falls Trail is located in Horsetooth Mountain Park. Take Harmony Road west until it reaches Taft Hill Road. Here Harmony Road becomes County Road 38E, continue straight. Follow County Road 38E around the south end of Horsetooth Reservoir, and at the top of the second hill, watch for the park entrance on the right. Take the Soderberg Trail for about .33 miles to the Horsetooth Falls Trail.

Horsetooth Rock

Length (one way)	1.25 miles (2.01 kilometers)
Elevation change	747 feet
Difficulty	Moderate
Season	All year
Suitability	Hiking, mountain biking, horseback riding
Usage	High
Restrictions	Park permit required Pets must be on a leash
Nearest trailhead	Park entrance

The Horsetooth Rock Trail is located in Horsetooth Mountain Park and provides the main access to Horsetooth Rock. It begins from the Soderberg Trail after a hike of about .9 miles from the park entrance. The trail begins at an elevation of 6,193 feet and makes a steady, moderate climb to

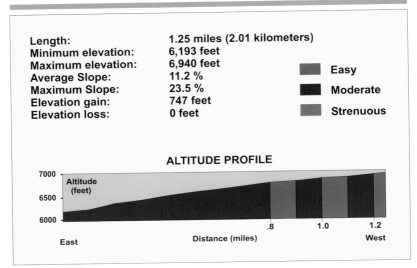

Length:	1.25 miles (2.01 kilometers)
Minimum elevation:	6,193 feet
Maximum elevation:	6,940 feet
Average Slope:	11.2 %
Maximum Slope:	23.5 %
Elevation gain:	747 feet
Elevation loss:	0 feet

Easy
Moderate
Strenuous

ALTITUDE PROFILE

Altitude (feet)

7000
6500
6000

.8   1.0   1.2

East   Distance (miles)   West

6,940 feet at the base of the rock. It travels through stands of ponderosa pines and makes a few switchbacks along the way. You get great views of Fort Collins and Horsetooth Reservoir

Here the trail climbs over a series of wooden steps as it makes its way to the base of Horsetooth Rock.

at the top and a few places along the trail. This is a popular access trail for climbing Horsetooth Rock and can be crowded on weekends.

Many places along the trail offer breathtaking views of Horsetooth Reservoir and the plains to the east.

Directions:

The Horsetooth Rock Trail is located in Horsetooth Mountain Park. Take Harmony Road west until it reaches Taft Hill Road. Here Harmony Road becomes County Road 38E, continue straight. Follow County Road 38E around the south end of Horsetooth Reservoir, and at the top of the second hill, watch for the park entrance on the right. Take the Soderberg Trail for about .9 miles to the Horsetooth Rock Trail.

Length (one way)	1.28 miles (2.05 kilometers)
Elevation change	496 feet
Difficulty	Easy to moderate
Season	All year
Suitability	Hiking, mountain biking, horseback riding
Usage	Low to moderate
Restrictions	Park permit required Pets must be on a leash
Nearest trailhead	Park entrance

The Loggers Trail is located in Horsetooth Mountain Park. It leaves the Mill Creek Trail on the north and travels south for 1.28 miles to intersect the service road. The first part of the trail makes a short, moderate descent through ponderosa pines. It levels out and continues south along the ridge. You get great views of Horsetooth Reservoir and Fort Collins all

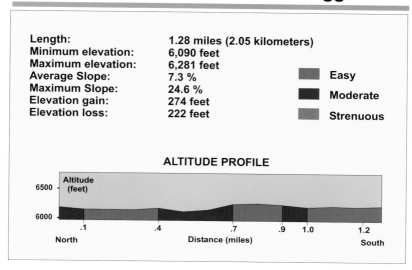

Length: 1.28 miles (2.05 kilometers)
Minimum elevation: 6,090 feet
Maximum elevation: 6,281 feet
Average Slope: 7.3 %
Maximum Slope: 24.6 %
Elevation gain: 274 feet
Elevation loss: 222 feet

Easy
Moderate
Strenuous

ALTITUDE PROFILE

Altitude (feet)

6500

6000

.1   .4   .7   .9   1.0   1.2

North   Distance (miles)   South

along the trail. At one point it makes a moderate climb for about .1 miles. As it nears the top, it levels out and follows an old road bed. Here it intersects the Carey Springs Trail after about three quarters of a mile and the Sawmill Trail about a quarter mile farther. This trail is easy to hike and offers great views.

Ponderosa pine and douglas fir provide welcome shade on a hot day.

This portion of the trail is easy to hike.

Directions:

The Loggers Trail is located in Horsetooth Mountain Park. Take Harmony Road west until it reaches Taft Hill Road. Here Harmony Road becomes County Road 38E, continue straight. Follow County Road 38E around the south end of Horsetooth Reservoir, and at the top of the second hill, watch for the park entrance on the right. Take the Soderberg Trail for about 1.4 miles to the Spring Creek Trail. Continue north for .55 miles to the Herrington Trail. Follow the Herrington Trail for .8 miles to the Loggers Trail.

Length (one way)	2.91 miles (4.69 kilometers)
Elevation change	1,140 feet
Difficulty	Moderate
Season	All year
Suitability	Hiking, mountain biking, horseback riding
Usage	Moderate
Restrictions	Park permit required Pets must be on a leash
Nearest trailhead	Park entrance

  The Mill Creek Trail is located in Horsetooth Mountain Park. It begins on a ridge in Lory State Park, about a half mile from the Arthur's Rock Parking Area on the Mill Creek Link Trail. The trail travels a short distance down hill through a gate into Horsetooth Mountain Park. You continue to descend under a dense canopy of ponderosa pine into a gulch and make several switchbacks up the ridge to the south. The trail tops

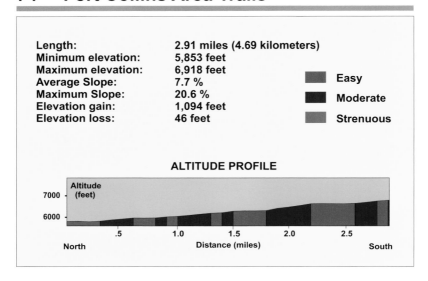

Length: 2.91 miles (4.69 kilometers)
Minimum elevation: 5,853 feet
Maximum elevation: 6,918 feet
Average Slope: 7.7 %   ▮ Easy
Maximum Slope: 20.6 %   ▮ Moderate
Elevation gain: 1,094 feet
Elevation loss: 46 feet   ▮ Strenuous

ALTITUDE PROFILE

this ridge and then travels down into Mill Creek Canyon and up the other side. Watch out for poison ivy in spots along the way. Once up out of the canyon you get great views of Horsetooth

Reservoir and Fort Collins. It levels off here and continues south to its intersection with the Loggers Trail. This is a good spot for a rest near a large rock under the shade of ponderosa pine trees.

Rusty takes a well deserved rest where the Mill Creek Trail meets the service road.

From the intersection, the trail makes a moderate climb up the ridge to the west. It winds its way north and west offering great views to the east. As you get higher, ponderosa pines give way to douglas fir trees. The trail intersects the service road on top of the ridge. From here you may access the Westridge or Spring Creek trails. The trail gains about 1,100 feet elevation in 2.9

miles. About 49% of this trail is of moderate difficulty. The rest is relatively easy.

Gorgeous views of Horsetooth Reservoir and Fort Collins are found along the upper reaches of the Mill Creek Trail.

Directions:

The Mill Creek Trail is located in Horsetooth Mountain Park. Take Harmony Road west until it reaches Taft Hill Road. Here Harmony Road becomes County Road 38E, continue straight. Follow County Road 38E around the south end of Horsetooth Reservoir, and at the top of the second hill, watch for the park entrance on the right. Take the Soderberg Trail for about 1.4 miles to the Spring Creek Trail. Continue north for .55 miles to the Herrington Trail. Follow the Herrington Trail for .8 miles to the Loggers Trail. Continue north on the Loggers Trail for about 1.1 miles to the Mill Creek Trail. You can also reach this trail from Lory State Park via the Mill Creek Link Trail (about .5 miles).

Length (one way)	1.04 miles (1.68 kilometers)
Elevation change	193 feet
Difficulty	Easy
Season	All year
Suitability	Hiking, mountain biking, horseback riding
Usage	Low
Restrictions	Park permit required Pets must be on a leash
Nearest trailhead	Park entrance

     The Nomad Trail is located in Horsetooth Mountain Park and connects the South Valley Trail in Lory State Park with the service road in Horsetooth Mountain Park. This trail is a short trail and easy to hike or ride. It begins on the north at an elevation of 5,512 feet and makes a gently rolling path south across the open grasslands to the service road at an elevation

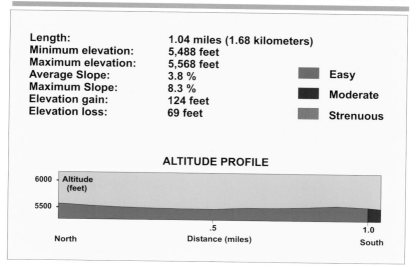

Length: 1.04 miles (1.68 kilometers)
Minimum elevation: 5,488 feet
Maximum elevation: 5,568 feet
Average Slope: 3.8 %   Easy
Maximum Slope: 8.3 %
Elevation gain: 124 feet   Moderate
Elevation loss: 69 feet
                                   Strenuous

ALTITUDE PROFILE

6000 - Altitude
       (feet)

5500 -

                    .5   1.0
     North   Distance (miles)   South

of 5,568 feet. There are watering tanks to the west of the trail but they don't always have water in them. The trail travels up

Here the trail passes by a large inlet of Horsetooth Reservoir.

and down a total of 193 feet in a little over a mile. This trail intersects the Sawmill Trail about .3 miles from its northern end. You get good views of the red rock formations to the east as well as the forested hillsides to the west.

This waterhole is located near the southern end of the Nomad Trail.

Directions:

The Nomad Trail is located in Horsetooth Mountain Park. Take Harmony Road west until it reaches Taft Hill Road. Here Harmony Road becomes County Road 38E, continue straight. Follow County Road 38E around the south end of Horsetooth Reservoir, and at the top of the second hill, watch for the park entrance on the right. Take the Soderberg Trail for about 1.4 miles to the Spring Creek Trail. Continue north for .55 miles to the Herrington Trail. Follow the Herrington Trail for .8 miles to the Loggers Trail. Continue north on the Loggers Trail for a short distance to the Sawmill Trail. Take the Sawmill Trail east for 1.2 miles to the Nomad Trail. The Nomad Trail can also be reached from Lory State Park via the South Valley Trail (about one mile).

Length (one way)	1.15 miles (1.85 kilometers)
Elevation change	677 feet
Difficulty	Moderate
Season	All year
Suitability	Hiking, mountain biking, horseback riding
Usage	Low to moderate
Restrictions	Park permit required Pets must be on a leash
Nearest trailhead	Park entrance

The Sawmill Trail is located in Horsetooth Mountain Park. It begins on the east end from the Nomad Trail at an elevation of 5,553 feet. It travels a short distance over the grassland before beginning a moderate climb up the foothills to the west. The trail winds its way up through the shrublands to

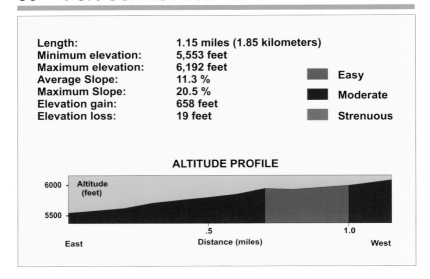

intersect the Loggers Trail at 6,192 feet. It intersects the Stout Trail about .1 miles from its western end. The upper reaches of the trail follows an old road. You'll pass an old shack on the

Bikers and horsemen should dismount here and walk over this rough section of the trail.

right near the west end of the trail. The Sawmill Trail is 1.15 miles in length and mostly moderate in difficulty.

The Sawmill Trail leaves the Nomad Trail and travels west into the foothills.

Directions:

The Sawmill Trail is located in Horsetooth Mountain Park. Take Harmony Road west until it reaches Taft Hill Road. Here Harmony Road becomes County Road 38E, continue straight. Follow County Road 38E around the south end of Horsetooth Reservoir, and at the top of the second hill, watch for the park entrance on the right. Take the Soderberg Trail for about 1.4 miles to the Spring Creek Trail. Continue north for .55 miles to the Herrington Trail. Follow the Herrington Trail for .8 miles to the Loggers Trail. Continue north on the Loggers Trail for a short distance to the Sawmill Trail.

Length (one way)	1.38 miles (2.22 kilometers)
Elevation change	543 feet
Difficulty	Easy to moderate
Season	All year
Suitability	Hiking, mountain biking, horseback riding
Usage	Moderate
Restrictions	Park permit required Pets must be on a leash
Nearest trailhead	Park entrance

The Soderberg Trail is located in Horsetooth Mountain Park and provides access to the Horsetooth Falls, Horsetooth Rock, and Spring Creek trails. It begins from the park entrance at an elevation of 5,812 feet and ends at the Spring Creek Trail at about 6,070 feet. The trail is mostly easy to hike as it climbs through 6,200 feet before descending to the Spring Creek Trail. It heads east from the parking area and winds around the east

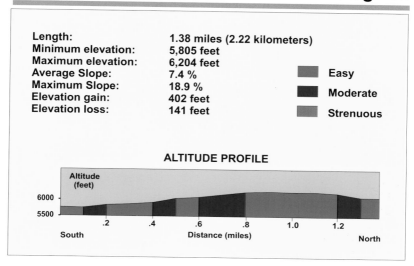

Length: 1.38 miles (2.22 kilometers)
Minimum elevation: 5,805 feet
Maximum elevation: 6,204 feet
Average Slope: 7.4 %   ■ Easy
Maximum Slope: 18.9 %
Elevation gain: 402 feet   ■ Moderate
Elevation loss: 141 feet
                                                              ■ Strenuous

ALTITUDE PROFILE

side of an open ridge before making a moderate climb to the
west. The trail passes the Horsetooth Falls Trail after about
.3 miles and continues climbing northwest until it intersects
the service road. It follows the service road for awhile before

Here the trail descends from the service road as it makes its way down to the
the parking area.

leaving it and heading toward the Horsetooth Rock Trail.

From here it contours the ridge before descending to the Spring Creek Trail. This trail offers great views of the valley below and is relatively easy to hike for most of its 1.4 miles.

The trail contours the ridge as it travels south from the Spring Creek Trail.

Directions:

The Soderberg Trail is located in Horsetooth Mountain Park. Take Harmony Road west until it reaches Taft Hill Road. Here Harmony Road becomes County Road 38E, continue straight. Follow County Road 38E around the south end of Horsetooth Reservoir, and at the top of the second hill, watch for the park entrance on the right. The trail begins from the northeast side of the parking area.

Length (one way)	2.17 miles (3.5 kilometers)
Elevation change	1,091 feet
Difficulty	Moderate
Season	All year
Suitability	Hiking, mountain biking, horseback riding
Usage	Low to moderate
Restrictions	Park permit required Pets must be on a leash
Nearest trailhead	Park entrance

The Spring Creek Trail parallels Spring Creek in Horsetooth Mountain Park. It begins from the Horsetooth Falls Trail at an elevation of 5,849 feet and climbs to the Westridge Trail at an elevation of 6,918 feet in about 2.2 miles. In addition, this trail intersects the Soderberg, Wathen, and Herrington trails along the way. There is a bench to rest and relax by a

Length:	2.17 miles (3.5 kilometers)
Minimum elevation:	5,849 feet
Maximum elevation:	6,918 feet
Average Slope:	9.5 %
Maximum Slope:	33.9 %
Elevation gain:	1,080 feet
Elevation loss:	11 feet

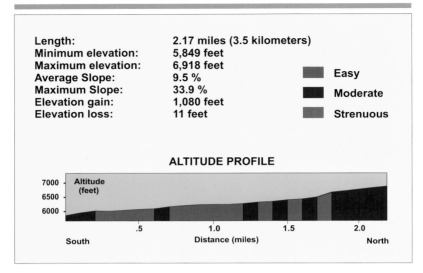

peaceful pool near the intersection with the Soderberg Trail. The trail travels through ponderosa pine stands and along a large meadow containing Spring Creek. About half of the trail

This bench sits beside Spring Creek, offering a cool rest on a hot summer's day.

is easy to hike with the rest being moderate to strenuous. The steepest part of the trail occurs as it approaches the Westridge

Trail on its northern end. The Spring Creek Trail gains about 1,080 feet in elevation along its length.

The trail makes a steep climb toward the servic road and the Westridge Trail.

Dircetions:

The Spring Creek Trail is located in Horsetooth Mountain Park. Take Harmony Road west until it reaches Taft Hill Road. Here Harmony Road becomes County Road 38E, continue straight. Follow County Road 38E around the south end of Horsetooth Reservoir, and at the top of the second hill, watch for the park entrance on the right. Take the Soderberg Trail for about 1.4 miles to the Spring Creek Trail.

Length (one way)	2.87 miles (4.51 kilometers)
Elevation change	1,132 feet
Difficulty	Easy to moderate
Season	All year
Suitability	Hiking, mountain biking, horseback riding
Usage	Low to moderate
Restrictions	Park permit required Pets must be on a leash
Nearest trailhead	Park entrance

   The Stout Trail is one of the longer trails in Horsetooth Mountain Park. It begins on the north from the Sawmill Trail at an elevation of 6,116 feet and travels south along the open hillside of the foothills. It makes a 2.9 mile loop through ponderosa pine stands as well as open hillsides. From the

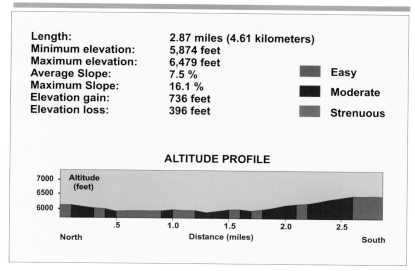

Length: 2.87 miles (4.61 kilometers)
Minimum elevation: 5,874 feet
Maximum elevation: 6,479 feet
Average Slope: 7.5 %
Maximum Slope: 16.1 %
Elevation gain: 736 feet
Elevation loss: 396 feet

Easy
Moderate
Strenuous

ALTITUDE PROFILE

Altitude (feet)

North   Distance (miles)   South

Sawmill Trail it travels south through ponderosa pine for .8 miles before intersecting the service road. From here it winds around the open foothills offering great views of Horsetooth

Horsetooth Rock comes into view as you travel on the southern portion of the Stout Trail.

Reservoir. At its southern most point it turns northwest and climbs the ridge toward the Herrington Trail. This is the most strenuous part of the trail. You get some good views of Horsetooth Rock just below its intersection with the Herrington Trail. Over half of the trail is of moderate difficulty with the

This is the most strenuous part of the trail as it climbs toward its intersection with the Herrington Trail.

rest being easy.

Directions:

The Stout Trail is located in Horsetooth Mountain Park. Take Harmony Road west until it reaches Taft Hill Road. Here Harmony Road becomes County Road 38E, continue straight. Follow County Road 38E around the south end of Horsetooth Reservoir, and at the top of the second hill, watch for the park entrance on the right. Take the Soderberg Trail for about 1.4 miles to the Spring Creek Trail. Continue north for .55 miles to the Herrington Trail. Take the Herrington Trail for about .3 miles to the Stout Trail.

Length (one way)	.96 miles (1.54 kilometers)
Elevation change	604 feet
Difficulty	Moderate
Season	All year
Suitability	Hiking, mountain biking, horseback riding
Usage	Moderate
Restrictions	Park permit required Pets must be on a leash
Nearest trailhead	Park entrance

The Wathen Trail is located in Horsetooth Mountain Park. It begins on the west near the base of Horsetooth Rock and travels downhill for about a mile to the Spring Creek Trail. Shortly down the trail there is a trail leading north to a horse watering tank. Those of you who ride horses in Horsetooth

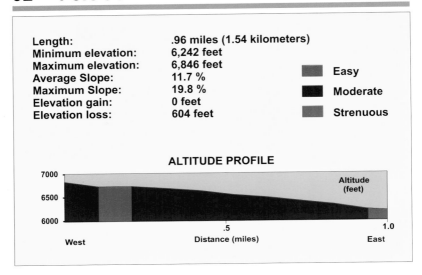

Length:	.96 miles (1.54 kilometers)
Minimum elevation:	6,242 feet
Maximum elevation:	6,846 feet
Average Slope:	11.7 %
Maximum Slope:	19.8 %
Elevation gain:	0 feet
Elevation loss:	604 feet

Easy
Moderate
Strenuous

ALTITUDE PROFILE

Altitude (feet)

7000
6500
6000

.5   1.0

West   Distance (miles)   East

Mountain Park should take advantage of this as water is scarce in the park. The trail winds its way down through ponderosa pine forest. There are some interesting rock formations near

This horse watering tank is located near the west end of the Wathen Trail.

the bottom of the trail. As you get close to the bottom you will travel through some lush meadows, just before you get to the

Spring Creek Trail. Eighty three percent of this mile long trail is of moderate difficulty.

Here the trail intersects with the Spring CreekTrail.

Directions:

The Wathen Trail is located in Horsetooth Mountain Park. Take Harmony Road west until it reaches Taft Hill Road. Here Harmony Road becomes County Road 38E, continue straight. Follow County Road 38E around the south end of Horsetooth Reservoir, and at the top of the second hill, watch for the park entrance on the right. Take the Soderberg Trail for about 1.4 miles to the Spring Creek Trail. Continue north for .44 miles to the Wathen Trail.

Length (one way)	1.71 miles (2.75 kilometers)
Elevation change	746 feet
Difficulty	Easy to moderate
Season	All year
Suitability	Hiking, mountain biking, horseback riding
Usage	Low to moderate
Restrictions	Park permit required Pets must be on a leash
Nearest trailhead	Park entrance

The Westridge Trail is located in Horsetooth Mountain Park. It begins on the north at the top of the service road and travels south below the radio and microwave towers. Traveling along the top of the ridge, you get great views to the east and west, including the back side of Horsetooth Rock and the Masonville Valley. At one point, it makes a steep climb

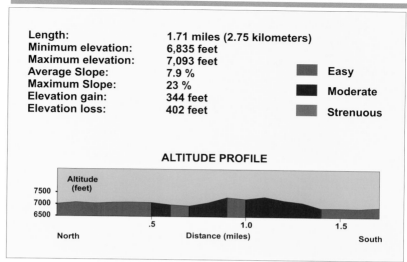

Length:	1.71 miles (2.75 kilometers)
Minimum elevation:	6,835 feet
Maximum elevation:	7,093 feet
Average Slope:	7.9 %
Maximum Slope:	23 %
Elevation gain:	344 feet
Elevation loss:	402 feet

Easy
Moderate
Strenuous

ALTITUDE PROFILE

over some wooden steps. Shortly beyond the steps you come to a point where you can see the back side of Horsetooth Rock and the Masonville Valley. The last part of the trail descends

If you look closely, you can see climbers standing on top of Horsetooth Rock as the Westridge Trail gives you a view from the west side.

along the east side of the ridge and passes below Horsetooth Rock. Here you get some up close and personal views of the rock. The trail travels up and down along the top of the west most ridge, gaining and losing a total of over 740 feet. This trail is mostly easy to hike with a few moderate sections along

The northern part of the trail travels beneath the radio towers on top of the ridge.

its 1.7 mile length.

Directions:

The Westridge Trail is located in Horsetooth Mountain Park. Take Harmony Road west until it reaches Taft Hill Road. Here Harmony Road becomes County Road 38E, continue straight. Follow County Road 38E around the south end of Horsetooth Reservoir, and at the top of the second hill, watch for the park entrance on the right. Take the Soderberg Trail for about .9 miles to the Horsetooth Rock Trail. Follow the Horsetooth Rock Trail for about 1.25 miles to the Westridge Trail.

Lory State Park

Lory State Park lies south of Bellvue and west of Horsetooth Reservoir. Its 2,500 acres lie in the transition zone between the plains and the foothills. There are approximately seventeen miles of trails within the park varying in difficulty from easy to moderate. About nine miles of trails are restricted to foot only traffic while the rest are available for foot, mountain bike, or horseback use. Elevations range from 5,400 to 7,000 feet. The park is popular with both mountain bikers and horseback riders. There is a riding stable (Double Diamond Stables) at the north end of the park and an equestrian jumping course at the south end. The Arthur's Rock Trail is the most popular trail in the park. Heavy foot traffic can be experienced during the warmer months of the year. This is a great area for wildflowers, wildlife, and scenic vistas. The trails here offer spectacular views of the red rock ridges runing the length of the park.

The park is open year round from dawn to dark (10 pm). A daily entrance permit or annual pass is required to use the park. Permits can be obtained at the visitors center just inside the park entrance.

Lory State Park Trails

TRAIL	LENGTH (one way)	DIFFICULTY	SUITABILITY
Arthur's Rock	1.69 miles	Moderate	Foot only
East Valley	2.02 miles	Easy	Foot, bicycle, horseback
Mill Creek Link	.77 miles	Moderate	Foot, bicycle, horseback
Overlook	1.15 miles	Moderate	Foot only
Shoreline	.70 miles	Easy to moderate	Foot, bicycle, horseback
South Valley	2.38 miles	Easy	Foot, bicycle, horseback
Timber	3.55 miles	Moderate	Foot only
Waterfall	.04 miles	Easy	Foot only
Well Gulch	1.34 miles	Easy to moderate	Foot only
Westridge	1.52 miles	Easy	Foot only
West Valley	2.0 miles	Easy	Foot, bicycle, horseback

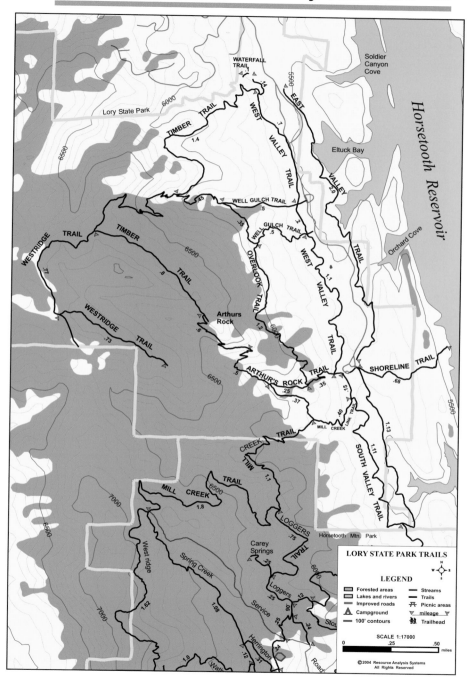

Arthur's Rock

Length (one way)	1.69 miles (2.72 kilometers)
Elevation change	1,072 feet
Difficulty	Moderate
Season	All year
Suitability	Foot only
Usage	High
Restrictions	Park permit required Pets must be on a leash
Nearest trailhead	Arthur's Rock Parking Area

The Arthur's Rock Trail is probably the most popular trail in Lory State Park. It makes a moderate climb for 1.7 miles to the base of Arthur's Rock, offering great views of Horsetooth Reservoir and the city of Fort Collins. The trail leaves the parking area at an elevation of 5,644 feet and ends at an elevation of 6,716 feet, intersecting the West Valley, Overlook, Mill Creek Link, and Timber trails along the way. It travels west up a narrow gulch, crossing a small stream several

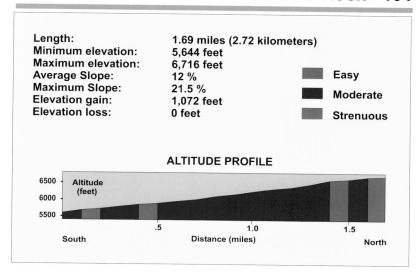

Length: 1.69 miles (2.72 kilometers)
Minimum elevation: 5,644 feet
Maximum elevation: 6,716 feet
Average Slope: 12 %   ▬ Easy
Maximum Slope: 21.5 %   ▬ Moderate
Elevation gain: 1,072 feet
Elevation loss: 0 feet   ▬ Strenuous

ALTITUDE PROFILE

Altitude (feet)

6500
6000
5500

.5   1.0   1.5

South   Distance (miles)   North

times. It then climbs the south side of the gulch via numerous switchbacks. After passing the Overlook Trail, it makes a gentle climb to the north through a large meadow. The trail

The trail travels behind Arthur's Rock as it climbs the ridge and then approaches the rock from the north.

gets steeper at the end of the meadow as it climbs toward Arthur's Rock. There are some vantage points here for taking in the views. The trail continues its climb behind some rocks and winds its way to its intersection with the Timber Trail. Follow the trail a short distance to the right to get to Arthur's Rock. Most of this trail is of moderate difficulty. There are a

Ponderosa pines have been ravaged by mountain pine beetles near the top of the trail.

few sections that some might consider strenuous. Horses and bikes are not permitted on this trail.

Directions:

The Arthur's Rock Trail is located in Lory State Park. Take Overland Trail north to Bingham Hill Rd. Turn left and travel west to County Road 23. Turn left and travel about 1.4 miles. Take a right on County Road 25G. Drive another 1.6 miles to the park entrance. Alternatively, take Centennial Drive to the north dam of Horsetooth Reservoir and then turn left onto County road 25G. Follow the main park road about 2.2 miles to its end at the Arthur's Rock Parking Area. The trail begins to the west.

Length (one way)	2.02 miles (3.26 kilometers)
Elevation change	355 feet
Difficulty	Easy
Season	All year
Suitability	Hiking, mountain biking, horseback riding
Usage	Moderate
Restrictions	Park permit required Pets must be on a leash
Nearest trailhead	Parking area near Double Diamond Stables

     The East Valley Trail is located in Lory State Park. It is a level trail running north-south for two miles just east of the main road through Lory State Park. It is accessed on the north from a parking area near the Double Diamond Stables and on the south from the Arthur's Rock Parking Area. From

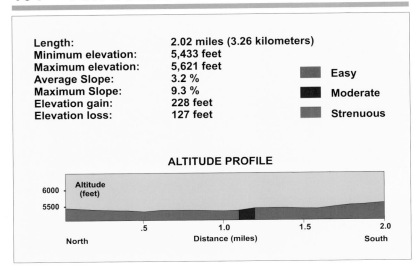

Length: 2.02 miles (3.26 kilometers)
Minimum elevation: 5,433 feet
Maximum elevation: 5,621 feet
Average Slope: 3.2 %
Maximum Slope: 9.3 %
Elevation gain: 228 feet
Elevation loss: 127 feet

Easy
Moderate
Strenuous

ALTITUDE PROFILE

Altitude (feet)

6000
5500

.5   1.0   1.5   2.0

North   Distance (miles)   South

the south, it travels in a northeast direction across open prairie. It crosses several gullies as it winds its way north. You may often see mule deer in the gullies. This trail gives you access

Wooden walkways are provided over wet areas.

via side trails to Orchard Cove and Eltuck Bay on Horsetooth Reservoir. It comes within a few hundred yards of these areas.

This trail provides a pleasant hike or ride along the valley in Lory State Park. It is a popular horseback riding trail.

The East Valley Trail is easy to hike or ride. It offers great views of the red rock formations west of Horsetooth Reservoir.

Directions:

The East Valley Trail is located in Lory State Park. Take Overland Trail north to Bingham Hill Rd. Turn left and travel west to County Road 23. Turn left and travel about 1.4 miles. Take a right on County Road 25G. Drive another 1.6 miles to the park entrance. Alternatively, take Centennial Drive to the north dam of Horsetooth Reservoir and then turn left onto County road 25G. Follow the main park road about .4 miles to a small parking area near the Double Diamond Stables. The trail begins just south of the parking area.

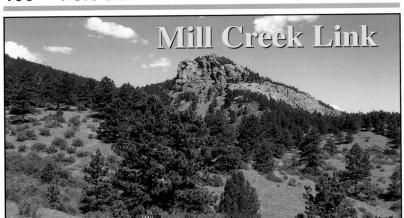

Length (one way)	.77 miles (1.24 kilometers)
Elevation change	367 feet
Difficulty	Moderate
Season	All year
Suitability	Hiking, mountain biking, horseback riding
Usage	Moderate
Restrictions	Park permit required Pets must be on a leash
Nearest trailhead	Arthur's Rock Parking Area

The Mill Creek Link Trail is located in Lory State Park. This trail provides access to the Mill Creek Trail leading into Horsetooth Mountain Park. The trail leaves the South Valley Trail just below the Arthur's Rock Parking Area and heads south for a short distance before climbing the shrub covered hillsides to the west. It is rocky and steep in spots as it approaches its intersection with the Mill Creek Trail. Horses

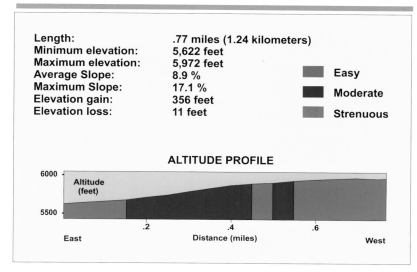

Length:	.77 miles (1.24 kilometers)
Minimum elevation:	5,622 feet
Maximum elevation:	5,972 feet
Average Slope:	8.9 %
Maximum Slope:	17.1 %
Elevation gain:	356 feet
Elevation loss:	11 feet

Easy

Moderate

Strenuous

ALTITUDE PROFILE

and bikes are only permitted on this trail to the Mill Creek Trail junction. From here the trail travels northwest making a moderate climb to its intersection with the Arthur's Rock

The trail makes a moderate climb up the brushy hillside on its way toward the Mill Creek Trail.

Trail in a large meadow. This trail offers an alternative way of traveling to or from Arthur's Rock.

A group of horsemen are enjoying their ride on a trail below the Mill Creek Link Trail.

Directions:

The Mill Creek Link Trail is located in Lory State Park. Take Overland Trail north to Bingham Hill Rd. Turn left and travel west to County Road 23. Turn left and travel about 1.4 miles. Take a right on County Road 25G. Drive another 1.6 miles to the park entrance. Alternatively, take Centennial Drive to the north dam of Horsetooth Reservoir and then turn left onto County road 25G. Follow the main park road about 2.2 miles to its end at the Arthur's Rock Parking Area. The trail begins from the South Valley Trail and travels southwest.

Length (one way)	1.15 miles (1.85 kilometers)
Elevation change	762 feet
Difficulty	Moderate
Season	All year
Suitability	Foot only
Usage	Moderate
Restrictions	Park permit required Pets must be on a leash
Nearest trailhead	Homestead Picnic Area

     The Overlook Trail is located in Lory State Park and makes a north-south path across the foothills below Arthur's Rock. This trail offers great views of Horsetooth Reservoir and the valley below from almost anywhere along its path. The trail begins on the north from the Well Gulch Trail about a half mile west of the Homestead Picnic Area. It makes a short, moderate climb before leveling off and heading across

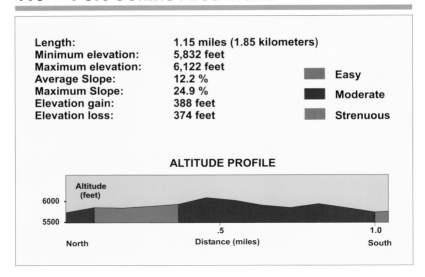

Length: 1.15 miles (1.85 kilometers)
Minimum elevation: 5,832 feet
Maximum elevation: 6,122 feet
Average Slope: 12.2 %   Easy
Maximum Slope: 24.9 %
Elevation gain: 388 feet   Moderate
Elevation loss: 374 feet
                                                       Strenuous

ALTITUDE PROFILE

Altitude
(feet)

6000

5500

                           .5   1.0
North   Distance (miles)   South

the open hillside to the south. There are numerous patches
of wildflowers along this section of the trail. About a third
of the way, the trail becomes more moderate in difficulty. It

The trail travels through ponderosa pine stands near its southern end.

travels up and down the hillside, gaining and losing over seven
hundred feet in elevation. Here it travels through ponderosa

pine stands offering welcome shade on a sunny day. The trail winds its way below Arthur's Rock and then descends to its intersection with the Arthur's Rock Trail. This 1.2 mile long

The trail travels below Arthur's Rock. This is a good place to rest before dropping down to the Arhtur's Rock Trail.

trail is a foot only trail. Horses and bikes are not permitted.

Directions:

The Overlook Trail is located in Lory State Park. Take Overland Trail north to Bingham Hill Rd. Turn left and travel west to County Road 23. Turn left and travel about 1.4 miles. Take a right on County Road 25G. Drive another 1.6 miles to the park entrance. Alternatively, take Centennial Drive to the north dam of Horsetooth Reservoir and then turn left onto County road 25G. Follow the main park road about 1.3 miles to the Homestead Picnic Area. Take the Well Gulch Trail about a half mile west to the north end of the Overlook Trail.

Shoreline

Length (one way)	.7 miles (1.12 kilometers)
Elevation change	319 feet
Difficulty	Easy to moderate
Season	All year
Suitability	Hiking, mountain biking, horseback riding
Usage	Low to moderate
Restrictions	Park permit required Pets must be on a leash
Nearest trailhead	Arthur's Rock Parking Area

The Shoreline Trail is located in Lory State Park. It travels east from the Arthur's Rock Parking Area for about three quarters of a mile to the west shore of Horsetooth Reservoir. It makes an easy climb over the hogback to the east and then makes a moderate descent to the reservoir. The scenery is resplendent with many brush-covered ridges and knolls and

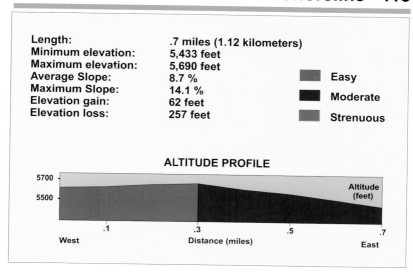

Length:	.7 miles (1.12 kilometers)
Minimum elevation:	5,433 feet
Maximum elevation:	5,690 feet
Average Slope:	8.7 %
Maximum Slope:	14.1 %
Elevation gain:	62 feet
Elevation loss:	257 feet

■ Easy
■ Moderate
■ Strenuous

ALTITUDE PROFILE

Altitude (feet)

West   Distance (miles)   East

lush green meadows. Deer might be seen in the evening and early morning hours. The ridge tops are lined with ponderosa pine. The trail gets a little rocky as you descend to the reservoir

The trail leaves the parking area toward the beautiful red rock formations.

but soon opens up into a beautiful meadow. It ends on a rocky beach near a grove of cottonwoods. This is a very nice spot for a picnic. This trail is relatively easy to hike.

Horsetooth Reservoir comes into view as the trail begins a descent through the rock formations.

Directions:

The Shoreline Trail is located in Lory State Park. Take Overland Trail north to Bingham Hill Rd. Turn left and travel west to County Road 23. Turn left and travel about 1.4 miles. Take a right on County Road 25G. Drive another 1.6 miles to the park entrance. Alternatively, take Centennial Drive to the north dam of Horsetooth Reservoir and then turn left onto County road 25G. Follow the main park road about 2.2 miles to its end at the Arthur's Rock Parking Area. The trail begins to the east of the parking area.

South Valley

Length (one way)	2.38 miles (3.84 kilometers)
Elevation change	458 feet
Difficulty	Easy
Season	All year
Suitability	Hiking, mountain biking, horseback riding
Usage	Moderate
Restrictions	Park permit required Pets must be on a leash
Nearest trailhead	Arthur's Rock Parking Area

The South Valley Trail begins from the Arthur's Rock Parking Area and makes a 2.4 mile loop to the Horsetooth Mountain Park Boundary and back. The trail winds its way south through the open, grassy area east of the foothills. You get great views of the foothills and the red rocks west of

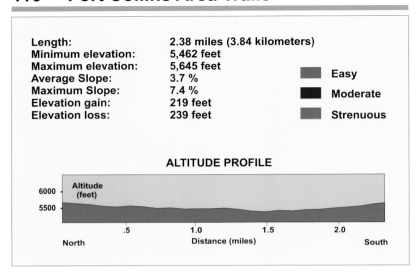

Length: 2.38 miles (3.84 kilometers)
Minimum elevation: 5,462 feet
Maximum elevation: 5,645 feet
Average Slope: 3.7 %   ■ Easy
Maximum Slope: 7.4 %   ■ Moderate
Elevation gain: 219 feet
Elevation loss: 239 feet   ■ Strenuous

ALTITUDE PROFILE

Horsetooth Reservoir. The trail passes through an equestrian jump area. It crosses a gulley just before you reach the Horsetooth Mountain Park Boundary and makes its way north,

The South Valley Trail makes a loop south through the equestrian jump course.

returning to the parking area. This recently reconstructed trail is easy to hike with some wooden bridges spanning a few gullies.   It is also great for mountain bikes and horseback riding.

Here the South Valley Trail leaves Horsetooth Mountain Park and travels north to the Arthur's Rock Parking Area.

Directions:

The South Valley Trail is located in Lory State Park. Take Overland Trail north to Bingham Hill Rd. Turn left and travel west to County Road 23. Turn left and travel about 1.4 miles. Take a right on County Road 25G. Drive another 1.6 miles to the park entrance. Alternatively, take Centennial Drive to the north dam of Horsetooth Reservoir and then turn left onto County road 25G. Follow the main park road about 2.2 miles to its end at the Arthur's Rock Parking Area. The trail begins to the south.

Timber

Length (one way)	3.55 miles (5.72 kilometers)
Elevation change	1,670 feet
Difficulty	Moderate
Season	All year
Suitability	Foot only
Usage	Moderate
Restrictions	Park permit required Pets must be on a leash
Nearest trailhead	Timber Group Picnic Area

The Timber Trail is the longest and one of the more strenuous trails in Lory State Park. It travels from the Timber Group Picnic Parking Area on the north to the Arthur's Rock Trail on the south, covering 3.55 miles. The trail intersects a cutoff trail to the Well Gulch Trail and the Westridge Trail along the way. Magnificent views of the valley below, Horsetooth Reservoir, and Fort Collins can be seen from various points

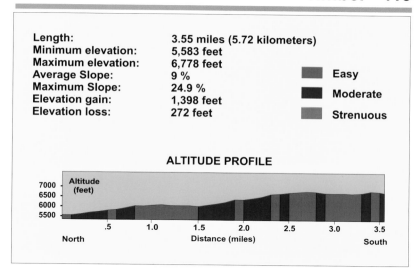

Length:	3.55 miles (5.72 kilometers)
Minimum elevation:	5,583 feet
Maximum elevation:	6,778 feet
Average Slope:	9 %
Maximum Slope:	24.9 %
Elevation gain:	1,398 feet
Elevation loss:	272 feet

Easy
Moderate
Strenuous

ALTITUDE PROFILE

along the trail. The trail leaves the parking area at an elevation of 5,583 feet and ends at the Arthur's Rock Trail at 6,710 feet, gaining almost 1,400 feet along the way. Surprisingly, over

The Timber Trail offers great opportunities for viewing wildflowers all along its length.

half of this trail is easy to hike. The rest is moderate to steep and is interspersed between easy stretches. The lower sections of this trail are home to rattlesnakes. Be on the lookout during the warmer times of the year. Look for mule deer on the lower slopes in the morning and evening hours. Many sections of

You get spectacular views of Horsetooth Reservoir and Fort Collins from the Timber Trail.

the trail have numerous wildflowers for your viewing pleasure. The Timber Trail is a foot only trail. Horses and bikes are not permitted.

Directions:

The Timber Trail is located in Lory State Park. Take Overland Trail north to Bingham Hill Rd. Turn left and travel west to County Road 23. Turn left and travel about 1.4 miles. Take a right on County Road 25G. Drive another 1.6 miles to the park entrance. Alternatively, take Centennial Drive to the north dam of Horsetooth Reservoir and then turn left onto County road 25G. Follow the main park road about a half mile to the Timber Group Picnic Parking Area. The trail leaves the south side of the parking area.

Length (one way)	.04 miles (.07 kilometers)
Elevation change	10 feet
Difficulty	Easy
Season	All year
Suitability	Foot only
Usage	Moderate
Restrictions	Park permit required Pets must be on a leash
Nearest trailhead	Timber Group Picnic Area

The Waterfall Trail is a very short trail leading to Soldier Canyon Falls in Lory State Park. The trail is less than a tenth of a mile long and is very easy to hike. It begins at the west end of the Timber Group Picnic Area and follows a small stream in a narrow gulch. It ends after crossing a wooden

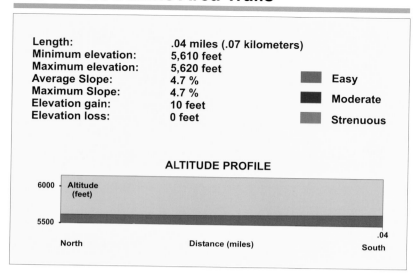

Length:	.04 miles (.07 kilometers)	
Minimum elevation:	5,610 feet	
Maximum elevation:	5,620 feet	
Average Slope:	4.7 %	Easy
Maximum Slope:	4.7 %	Moderate
Elevation gain:	10 feet	Strenuous
Elevation loss:	0 feet	

ALTITUDE PROFILE

bridge just below the falls. Soldier Canyon Falls is small but picturesque. This is a very pleasant walk with numerous birds singing along the trail.

The Waterfall Trail leaves from the west end of the Timber Group Picnic Area.

Soldier Canyon Falls is small but very picturesque.

Directions:

The Waterfall Trail is located in Lory State Park. Take Overland Trail north to Bingham Hill Rd. Turn left and travel west to County Road 23. Turn left and travel about 1.4 miles. Take a right on County Road 25G. Drive another 1.6 miles to the park entrance. Alternatively, take Centennial Drive to the north dam of Horsetooth Reservoir and then turn left onto County road 25G. Follow the main park road about a half mile to the Timber Group Picnic Parking Area. The trail leaves the west side of the parking area.

Length (one way)	1.34 miles (2.15 kilometers)
Elevation change	732 feet
Difficulty	Easy to moderate
Season	All year
Suitability	Foot only
Usage	Moderate
Restrictions	Park permit required Pets must be on a leash
Nearest trailhead	Well Gulch Trailhead

The Well Gulch Trail is a self-guided nature trail located in Lory State Park. It makes a loop up into the foothills and back to the main road through the park. There are numerous interpretive markers along its path. The trail begins from the main road at an elevation of 5,507 feet and ends at the Homestead Picnic Area at about the same elevation. It gains 370 feet in elevation before dropping back down to the main

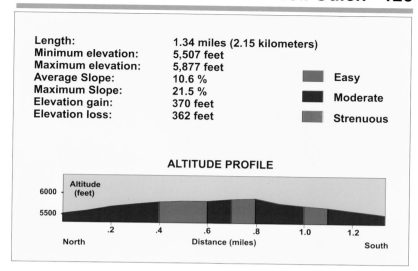

Length:	1.34 miles (2.15 kilometers)	
Minimum elevation:	5,507 feet	
Maximum elevation:	5,877 feet	
Average Slope:	10.6 %	Easy
Maximum Slope:	21.5 %	Moderate
Elevation gain:	370 feet	
Elevation loss:	362 feet	Strenuous

ALTITUDE PROFILE

road. The trail intersects the West Valley and Overlook trails along the way. From its north end, the trail travels west through the narrow Well Gulch. The trail can be wet and muddy in

After travelling up Well Gulch, the trail turns south through a ponderosa pine stand.

spots in years with high spring runoff. After traveling through a meadow, the trail turns south and makes a moderate climb through a ponderosa pine stand. It passes the Overlook Trail and heads east, descending through a narrow gulch. From here the trail winds its way down through open areas to the

Here the Well Gulch Trail approaches the Homestead Picnic Area.

Homestead Picnic Area. It is a short walk up the main road to the starting point. Seventy percent of this 1.3 mile long trail is of moderate difficulty. Horses and bikes are not permitted on this foot only trail.

Directions:

The Well Gulch Trail is located in Lory State Park. Take Overland Trail north to Bingham Hill Rd. Turn left and travel west to County Road 23. Turn left and travel about 1.4 miles. Take a right on County Road 25G. Drive another 1.6 miles to the park entrance. Alternatively, take Centennial Drive to the north dam of Horsetooth Reservoir and then turn left onto County road 25G. Follow the main park road about 1.1 miles to the beginning of the trail. Parking is on the east side of the road.

Length (one way)	1.52 miles (2.45 kilometers)
Elevation change	547 feet
Difficulty	Easy
Season	All year
Suitability	Foot only
Usage	Low
Restrictions	Park permit required Pets must be on a leash
Nearest trailhead	Arthur's Rock Parking Area

The Westridge Trail is located in the western section of Lory State Park. This trail is easy to hike and offers great views of the valley to the west of the park. Unfortunately, you must hike two to three miles to get to it. The trail leaves the Timber Trail at an elevation of 6,696 feet and follows an

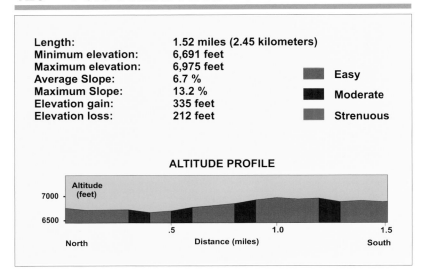

Length:	1.52 miles (2.45 kilometers)
Minimum elevation:	6,691 feet
Maximum elevation:	6,975 feet
Average Slope:	6.7 %
Maximum Slope:	13.2 %
Elevation gain:	335 feet
Elevation loss:	212 feet

■ Easy
■ Moderate
■ Strenuous

ALTITUDE PROFILE

Altitude (feet)

7000

6500

.5   1.0   1.5

North   Distance (miles)   South

old road to the southwest. It passes through a ponderosa pine/ douglas fir forest offering ample shade. This pleasant walk travels through several meadows before turning south along

It's an easy walk through these meadows along the Westridge Trail.

the ridge. From here it makes a moderate to steep climb along the ridge. You get a good view of the valley to the west and the radio towers to the south. This little used trail is a foot only trail and is about 1.5 miles long.

You get a great view of the Masonville Valley and the radio towers to the south from the Westridge Trail.

Directions:

The Westridge Trail is located in Lory State Park. Take Overland Trail north to Bingham Hill Rd. Turn left and travel west to County Road 23. Turn left and travel about 1.4 miles. Take a right on County Road 25G. Drive another 1.6 miles to the park entrance. Alternatively, take Centennial Drive to the north dam of Horsetooth Reservoir and then turn left onto County road 25G. Follow the main park road about 2.2 miles to its end at the Arthur's Rock parking area. Take the Arthur's Rock Trail for 1.7 miles to the Timber Trail. Continue north on the Timber Trail for about .8 miles to the Westridge Trail.

Length (one way)	2.0 miles (323 kilometers)
Elevation change	347 feet
Difficulty	Easy
Season	All year
Suitability	Hiking, mountain biking, horseback riding
Usage	Moderate
Restrictions	Park permit required Pets must be on a leash
Nearest trailhead	Timber Group Picnic Area Arthur's Rock Parking Area

The West Valley Trail runs north-south along the west side of the valley in Lory State Park. It begins near the Timber Group Picnic Area and travels south to the Arthur's Rock Trail. The Timber Trail also begins here but soon splits off to the west up the ridge. After climbing the ridge for a short time, the West Valley Trail drops down close to the main road. Here

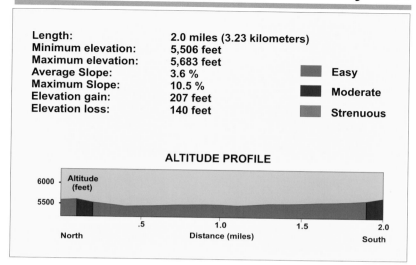

Length:	2.0 miles (3.23 kilometers)
Minimum elevation:	5,506 feet
Maximum elevation:	5,683 feet
Average Slope:	3.6 %
Maximum Slope:	10.5 %
Elevation gain:	207 feet
Elevation loss:	140 feet

Easy
Moderate
Strenuous

ALTITUDE PROFILE

it parallels the road. It passes just behind and to the west of the Homestead Picnic Area. This trail is generally wide open offering good visibility. There are, however, a few gullies

The south end of the West Valley Trail intersects the Arthur's Rock Trail near the parking area.

where horsemen or bikers could surprise one another. It is best to be cautious when passing through these areas. This easy hike intersects the Arthur's Rock Trail just west of the parking area. The West Valley Trail is very popular with mountain

The West Valley Trail is a good trail for viewing wildflowers.

bikers as well as horseback riders.

Directions:

The West Valley Trail is located in Lory State Park. Take Overland Trail north to Bingham Hill Rd. Turn left and travel west to County Road 23. Turn left and travel about 1.4 miles. Take a right on County Road 25G. Drive another 1.6 miles to the park entrance. Alternatively, take Centennial Drive to the north dam of Horsetooth Reservoir and then turn left onto County road 25G. Follow the main park road about a half mile to the Timber Group Picnic Parking Area. Take the Timber Trail at the south side of the parking area for .1 miles to the West Valley Trail.

Length (one way)	10.35 miles (16.66 kilometers)
Elevation change	308 feet
Difficulty	Easy
Season	All year
Suitability	Hiking, biking, roller blading
Usage	Moderate
Restrictions	Pets must be on a leash
Nearest trailhead	Boyd Lake State Park, Seven Lakes, Barnes, Centennial parks

The Loveland Recreation Trail is a ten foot wide concrete path that extends from the north end of Boyd Lake south and west to Wilson Avenue near the yard waste recycling center. The trail begins from Road 11C near the north end of Boyd Lake. There is no parking here. The nearest parking is in Boyd Lake State Park (fee required) or Seven Lakes Park. The trail winds its way south through Boyd Lake State Park offering great views of the lake and access to facilities in the park. It passes through the seven lakes area along the east

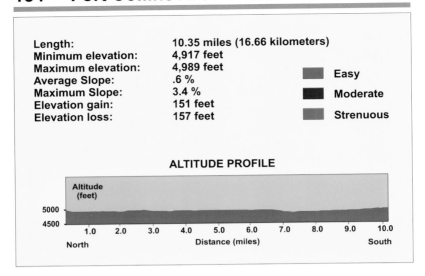

Length:	10.35 miles (16.66 kilometers)
Minimum elevation:	4,917 feet
Maximum elevation:	4,989 feet
Average Slope:	.6 %
Maximum Slope:	3.4 %
Elevation gain:	151 feet
Elevation loss:	157 feet

Easy
Moderate
Strenuous

ALTITUDE PROFILE

edge of Seven Lakes Park. From here it continues south where it follows the Chubbuck Ditch and passes under Eisenhower Boulevard. It travels southwest, crossing Boise and Madison avenues, to the city Civic Center. After traveling south on Washington Avenue a few blocks, it picks up again and turns northwest, passing through the old fairgrounds and

Experience the beauty of the Big Thompson River from the southern section of the trail.

Barnes Park. The trail follows the Big Thompson River, passing through Centennial Park. This section of the trail is quite beautiful, offering fishing and wildlife viewing. The Loveland Recreation Trail is level and great for hiking, riding, roller blading, or just taking a leisurely stroll through Boyd Lake State Park or along the Big Thompson River.

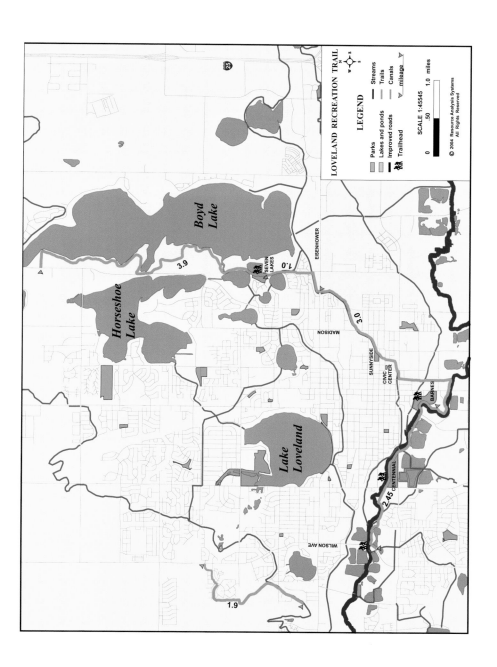

LOVELAND RECREATION TRAIL

LEGEND

Parks	— Streams	
Lakes and ponds	— Trails	
Improved roads	— Canals	
Trailhead	▽— mileage	

SCALE 1:45545

0   .50   1.0 miles

© 2004 Resource Analysis Systems
All Rights Reserved

Boyd Lake

Horseshoe Lake

Lake Loveland

EISENHOWER

MADISON

SUNNYSIDE

CIVIC CENTER

BARNES

CENTENNIAL

WILSON AVE

SEVEN LAKES

3.9

1.0

3.0

2.45

1.9

25

Plans are to eventually extend the trail completely around the city in a large circle. Various pieces have been completed. The largest is a two mile section traveling from

The trail travels through Boyd Lake State Park offering you great views of the lake.

35th Street and Wilson Avenue through a housing area and south to a bridge over a canal.

Directions:

The Loveland Recreation Trail is located in the city of Loveland. Its primary access points are Boyd Lake State Park, Seven Lakes Park, Barnes Park, Centennial Park, and Wilson Avenue north of the yard waste recycling center. Take Madison Avenue and Road 11C north from Eisenhower Blvd. to Boyd Lake State Park. Take Boise Avenue north from Eisenhower Blvd. and Park St. east to Seven Lakes Park. Take Hwy 287 south from Eisenhower Blvd. to Barnes Park near the old fairgrounds. Take Taft Avenue south from Eisenhower Blvd. to Centennial Park.

Length	7 miles (11.26 kilometers)
Difficulty	Easy
Season	All year
Suitability	Hiking, mountain biking, horseback riding
Usage	Moderate
Restrictions	Pets must be on a leash
Nearest trailhead	Dixon Reservoir, Cottonwood Glen Park, Horsetooth Road

The Pineridge Natural Area is an ideal area for hiking, horseback riding, and mountain bike riding. There are seven named trails in the area totaling seven miles in length. These trails include: Ridge Trail, Park Trail, South Loop Trail, Timber Trail, Valley Trail, Reservoir Trail, and Viewpoint Trail. The majority of the trails are easy to hike. There are, however, a few spots that may require a moderate climb. This is a great area for wildlife viewing, offering potential sightings

The Timber Trail is a popular mountain bike trail and is generally wetter than the other trails.

of deer, prairie dogs, rabbits, and numerous species of birds. Fishing is available at Dixon Reservoir. There is a dog park for exercising your dog.

Ridge Trail: This trail travels from the dog park west and north along the first ridge to Cottonwood Glen Park.

Park Trail: This trail follows a road from Cottonwood Glen Park to the dog park.

South Loop Trail: This trail connects the Valley Trail with the Timber Trail making a loop through the south end of the natural area.

Timber Trail: This trail travels along the west most ridge of the natural area for about a mile. The Timber Trail is generally more wet than the other trails.

Valley Trail: This trail travels north-south along the valley floor. A large prairie dog town is located near the trail.

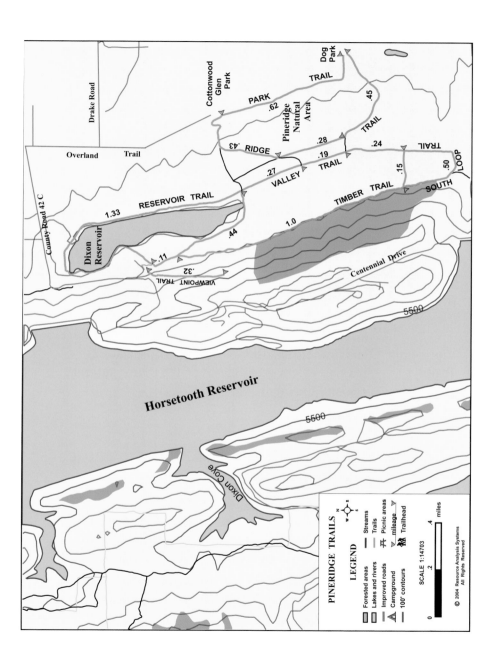

Reservoir   This trail makes a loop around Dixon Reservoir.
Trail: This easy hike offers access for fishing around the

There is easy access to Dixon Reservoir for fishing from the Reservoir Trail.

reservoir.

Viewpoint   This trail climbs the west ridge of the natural
Trail: area and offers great views of the entire natural
             area and the city.

Directions:

The Pineridge Natural Area trails are located on the west side of Fort Collins. The trails can be accessed from the west end of Horsetooth Road, Dixon Reservoir, and Cottonwood Glen Park. Take Drake Road west to Overland Trail. Turn north on Overland Trail to County Road 42C (just south of the CSU stadium). Travel west on County Road 42C for about .6 miles to the parking area above Dixon Reservoir. Alternatively, turn south on Overland Trail to Cottonwood Glen Park.

Length (one way)	1.4 miles (2.23 kilometers)
Elevation change	121 feet
Difficulty	Easy
Season	All year
Suitability	Hiking, mountain biking
Usage	Low
Restrictions	Pets must be on a leash
Nearest trailhead	Lions Park

The Pleasant Valley Trail is a paved (asphalt) trail that begins from Lions Park in Laporte and travels to Rist Canyon Road near Bellvue. The trail travels along the Poudre River until reaching the Cache La Poudre School. Here it turns north along the edge of the athletic fields. The trail turns west upon reaching County Road 54G and follows closely along the south edge of this highway. This trail currently ends at Galway Drive but a short section continues behind a barrier to Rist Canyon Road. An additional mile of trail is planned

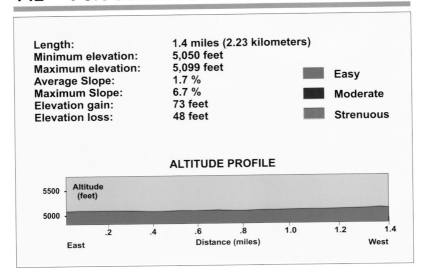

Length:	1.4 miles (2.23 kilometers)
Minimum elevation:	5,050 feet
Maximum elevation:	5,099 feet
Average Slope:	1.7 %
Maximum Slope:	6.7 %
Elevation gain:	73 feet
Elevation loss:	48 feet

Easy
Moderate
Strenuous

ALTITUDE PROFILE

Altitude (feet)

5500
5000

.2   .4   .6   .8   1.0   1.2   1.4

East   Distance (miles)   West

along Rist Canyon Road to the Poudre River and then north to Watson Lake. This section is expected to be completed by winter of 2005. The Pleasant Valley Trail is good for hiking, biking, and rollerblading but not for horseback riding as the traffic on County Road 54G is very heavy.

The trail travels north along the busy County Road 54G.

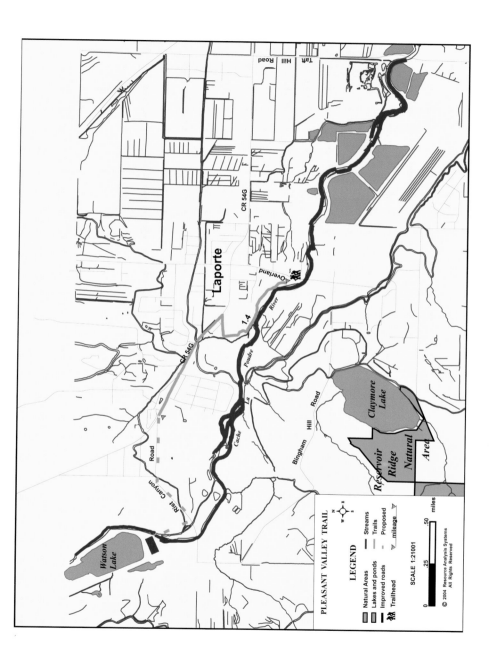

LEGEND

PLEASANT VALLEY TRAIL

Natural Areas
Lakes and ponds
Improved roads
Trailhead

Streams
Trails
Proposed
mileage

SCALE 1:21001

0   25   .50   miles

© 2004 Resource Analysis Systems
All Rights Reserved

There is access for fishing in the Poudre River near Lions Park.

Directions:

Take Highway 287 and County Road 54G from Fort Collins to Laporte. Turn south on Overland at the stop light. Travel about .3 miles to Lions Park. The Pleasant Valley Trail begins from the parking area on the west side of Overland.

Length (one way)	10 miles (16.1 kilometers)
Elevation change	347 feet
Difficulty	Easy
Season	All year
Suitability	Hiking, mountain biking, horseback riding
Usage	High
Restrictions	Pets must be on a leash
Nearest trailhead	Lions Park Taft Hill Road Enviornmental Learning Center

The Poudre River Trail is a paved trail that follows the Poudre River for about ten miles. It begins from Lions Park in Laporte and ends at the CSU Environmental Learning Center in east Fort Collins. This popular trail sees heavy use most of the year. Although horses are permitted on the trail, the first three miles are best as there is a dirt path running along side of the paved trail. There are numerous access points along the

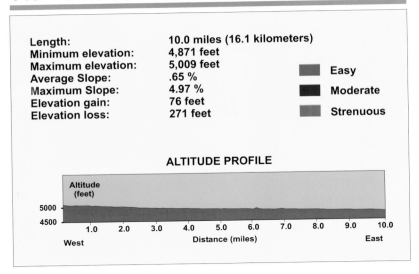

Length: 10.0 miles (16.1 kilometers)
Minimum elevation: 4,871 feet
Maximum elevation: 5,009 feet
Average Slope: .65 %   Easy
Maximum Slope: 4.97 %   Moderate
Elevation gain: 76 feet
Elevation loss: 271 feet   Strenuous

ALTITUDE PROFILE

Altitude
(feet)

5000
4500

1.0   2.0   3.0   4.0   5.0   6.0   7.0   8.0   9.0   10.0

West   Distance (miles)   East

trail making it easy to ride or hike as much as you want. Some of these include: Lions Park, Taft Hill Road, Lee Martinez Park, Northside Aztlan Community Center, Mulberry and Lemay, Timberline, Prospect, and the Environmental Learning Center.

There are a few air stations along the trail for bicyclists that need air for their tires.

There are benches, picnic tables, and air stations (for bicycle tires) at various points along the trail as well as a few drinking fountains. Good access is available to the Poudre River for fishing and wildlife viewing. The trail travels under most busy streets. You get to see parts of Fort Collins that you don't normally see. Although not completely free from traffic noise, the trail has a peaceful feeling to it, sort of like the "backcountry" of Fort Collins. The Poudre River

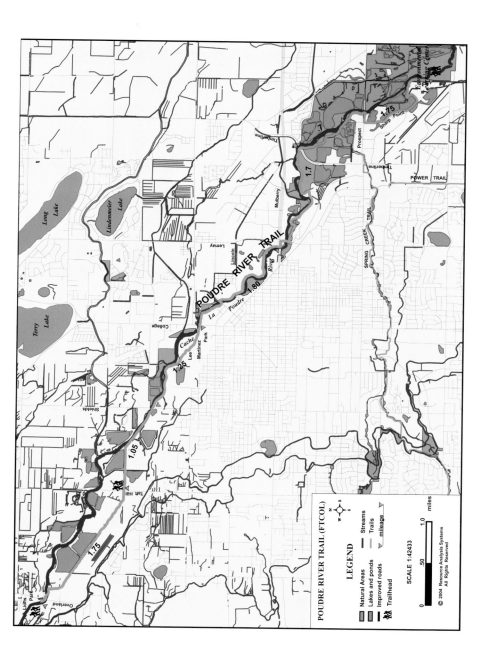

Trail is level and great for hiking, riding, roller blading, or just taking a leisurely stroll along the Poudre River.

Many sections of the trail offer a peaceful walk through nature.

The section from Lions Park to Taft Hill was completed in June of 2004.

Directions:

The Poudre River Trail is located in the city of Fort Collins. Its primary access points are Lions Park, North Taft Hill Road, Lee Martinez Park, and the Environmental Learning Center (ELC). Take Overland Trail to Lions Park. Take N. Taft Hill Road about a mile north of W. Vine Dr. to the parking area. There is a parking area on the east side of Lee Martinez Park just north of downtown Fort Collins. The Environmental Learning Center is located just north of E. Drake Road. Travel east on Drake Road, one mile past Timberline, turn left into the ELC just beyond the Municipal Water Treatment Plant.

Length (one way)	9.9 miles (15.93 kilometers)
Elevation change	148 feet
Difficulty	Easy
Season	All year -not maintained in winter
Suitability	Hiking, mountain biking, horseback riding
Usage	Moderate
Restrictions	Pets must be on a leash
Nearest trailhead	Kodak Trailhead 83rd Avenue Trailhead 71st Avenue Trailhead

The Poudre River Trail near Windsor is a ten foot wide ribbon of concrete that follows the Poudre River for 9.9 miles. The Trail offers non-motorized recreational opportunities including biking, walking, running, horseback riding, and rollerblading. It begins from a fence line southwest of Eastman

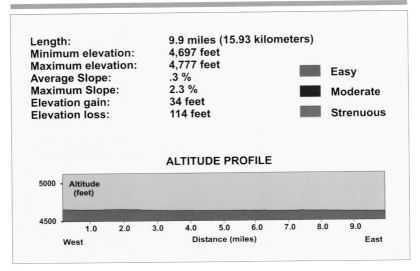

Length:	9.9 miles (15.93 kilometers)
Minimum elevation:	4,697 feet
Maximum elevation:	4,777 feet
Average Slope:	.3 %
Maximum Slope:	2.3 %
Elevation gain:	34 feet
Elevation loss:	114 feet

Easy
Moderate
Strenuous

ALTITUDE PROFILE

Altitude (feet)

5000

4500

1.0   2.0   3.0   4.0   5.0   6.0   7.0   8.0   9.0

Distance (miles)

West   East

Park and ends at 71st Avenue near Greeley. The trail winds its way around the north edge of the Water Valley housing development before crossing Highway 257 near the Kodak plant. It travels south to a trailhead near the river. From here it travels east for 5.4 miles to its intersection with 83rd Avenue. This section of the trail passes by the Poudre River Bluffs, an area where the land rises to over 200 feet above the river bottom. This is a great section of the trail offering many wildlife viewing opportunities. There is a parking area near 83rd Avenue.

The trail travels through a ranch where cattle may be present at certain times of the year.

The trail continues across 83rd Avenue and travels through a large meadow belonging to a ranch. There are three

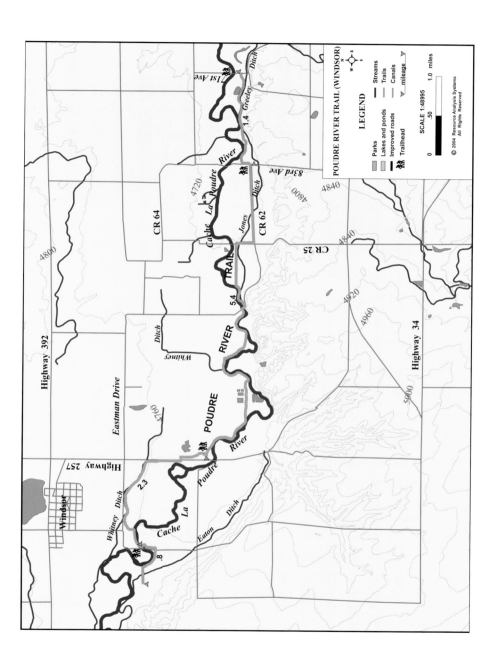

cattle guards to keep the ranch's cattle confined to specific pastures at certain times of the year. They consist of some fencing that form a narrow passage way requiring you to make two 90 degree turns and a 180 degree turn. The trail can be quite muddy and littered with manure when cattle are present.

Here the trail travels through the Poudre River Bluffs area.

After passing through the third cattle guard, the trail continues east below a steep bank and past a small lake to 71st Avenue.

Directions:

The Poudre River Trail (Windsor) can be accessed from four locations. Take Highway 392 east from Windsor to Highway 257. Travel south on 257 to Eastman Drive. Turn west on Eastman Drive and follow it past 7th Avenue to the southwest corner of Eastman Park. The trail travels along the south edge of the park. You may also access the trail from a trailhead just east of Highway 257 about a mile south of Eastman Drive. An alternative access is at 83rd Avenue and CR 62. Take Highway 392 east from Windsor to CR 27. Turn south and follow it to Bracewell. Turn east and follow the road until it becomes 83rd Avenue and crosses the Poudre River. CR 62 is a short distance south. The trailhead is a short distance west on CR 62. You can reach the 71st Avenue trailhead by turning east on 0 Street from 83rd Avenue just south of Bracewell. Continue east to 71st Avenue and turn south to the trailhead.

Length (one way)	1.73 miles (2.78 kilometers)
Elevation change	41 feet
Difficulty	Easy
Season	All year
Suitability	Hiking, biking
Usage	Low
Restrictions	Pets must be on a leash No motorized vehicles
Nearest trailhead	Riverside Drive

  The Power Trail is a 1.7 mile long trail that parallels a power line and railroad in east Fort Collins. This trail is paved, making it good for biking or roller blading. Runners enjoy the gravel path that runs along side the main trail most of the way. The trail begins just south of EPIC at a culdesac at the end of Riverside Drive. There are a few wiggles in the

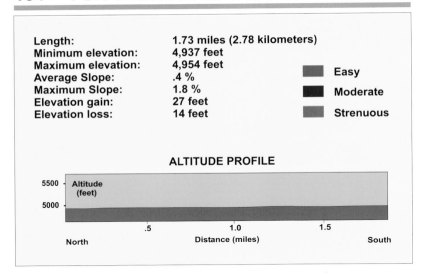

Length:	1.73 miles (2.78 kilometers)
Minimum elevation:	4,937 feet
Maximum elevation:	4,954 feet
Average Slope:	.4 %
Maximum Slope:	1.8 %
Elevation gain:	27 feet
Elevation loss:	14 feet

Easy
Moderate
Strenuous

ALTITUDE PROFILE

Altitude (feet)

5500
5000

.5   1.0   1.5

North   Distance (miles)   South

trail but it pretty much travels due south, crossing Drake and Horsetooth roads. There are several spur trails intersecting the Power Trail that provide access to housing developments along its path. The paved trail ends at Horsetooth Road just east of the Collindale Golf Course. A dirt road continues south along the railroad to Harmony Road. This trail is level and easy to

The Power Trail gets its name from the power lines that run along side it.

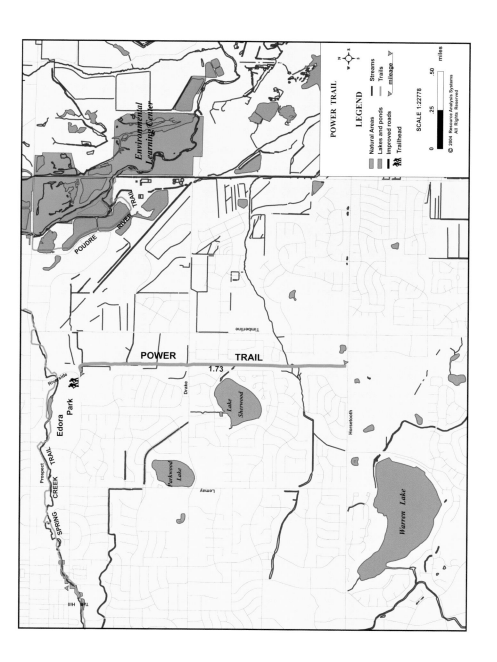

POWER TRAIL

LEGEND

Natural Areas
Lakes and ponds
Improved roads
Trailhead

Streams
Trails
mileage

SCALE 1:22778

0   .25   .50   miles

© 2004 Resource Analysis Systems
All Rights Reserved

Environmental Learning Center

POUDRE RIVER TRAIL

Timberline

POWER TRAIL

1.73

Riverside

Edora Park

Drake

Lake Sherwood

Prospect

SPRING CREEK TRAIL

Parkwood Lake

Lemay

Horsetooth

Warren Lake

hike or ride. Plans are to continue the trail from Horsetooth to Harmony roads.

There is a running path that travels along side the main trail.

Directions:

The Power Trail is located on the east side of Fort Collins. Take East Prospect to Riverside Ave. Turn south and follow Riverside Ave. to its end at a culdesac. This is the north end of the trail.

Length (one way)	4.87 miles (7.84 kilometers)
Elevation change	2,999 feet
Difficulty	Moderate
Season	All year
Suitability	Hiking, mountain biking, horseback riding
Usage	Low to moderate
Restrictions	Pets must be on a leash
Nearest trailhead	Round Mountain Trailhead

The Round Mountain National Trail System consists of the Summit Adventure Trail and the Foothills Nature Trail. Both trails offer interpretive markers along their entire length. Brochures for the nature trail are available at the beginning of the trail.

The nature trail begins at the parking area and travels along an old road bed above the Big Thompson River for a

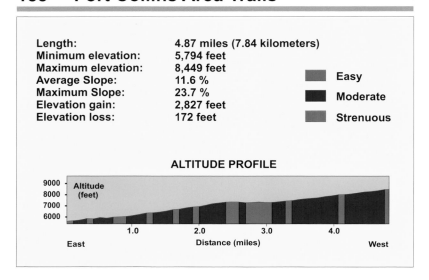

Length: 4.87 miles (7.84 kilometers)
Minimum elevation: 5,794 feet
Maximum elevation: 8,449 feet
Average Slope: 11.6 %   ▮ Easy
Maximum Slope: 23.7 %   ▮ Moderate
Elevation gain: 2,827 feet
Elevation loss: 172 feet   ▮ Strenuous

ALTITUDE PROFILE

short distance. The summit and nature trails split after about .2 miles. The nature trail offers an easy two mile walk (round trip)

This interesting rock formation stands in the middle of the trail.

along an old road with numerous interpretive markers along the way. The summit trail immediately begins a moderate climb to the south for about .1 miles. It then turns east and makes a steady climb along the hillside to the southeast. Great views of the canyon and river can be seen from the trail. After about a mile, the trail leaves the Big Thompson Canyon and travels up along a side canyon. It makes a moderate climb up a ridge above the side canyon through scattered ponderosa pine, douglas fir, and brushy areas. It then levels off and travels along a ledge-like path below large boulders and rock walls with

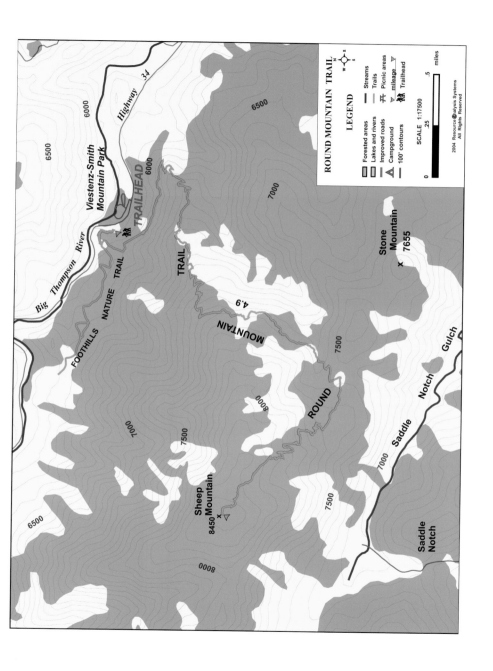

ROUND MOUNTAIN TRAIL

LEGEND

- Forested areas
- Lakes and rivers
- Improved roads
- ▲ Campground
- 100' contours
- Streams
- Trails
- ⊤ Picnic areas
- ▽ mileage
- Trailhead

SCALE 1:17500

0   .25   .5   miles

steep drop offs. The views here can be quite breathtaking.

Once past the rocky area, the trail descends into a gulch

The trail climbs above the Big Thompson Canyon offering spectacular views.

and begins a moderate climb through dense ground vegetation and scattered ponderosa pines toward the summit of Sheep Mountain. Great views of Pinewood Lake, Carter Lake, and the eastern plains can be seen along this stretch. At the summit you can see Longs Peak and Mount Meeker to the west.

Directions:

The Round Mountain Trail is located in the Big Thompson Canyon. Take Highway 34 west from Loveland. The Round Mountain Trailhead is on the left side of the road about four miles west of the Dam Store. The sign cannot be seen until you are right on top of it. The entrance to Viestenz-Smith Mountain Park is on the right just before the trailhead.

Shoshone

Length (one way)	1.5 miles (2.42 kilometers)
Elevation change	563 feet
Difficulty	Easy to moderate
Season	All year (sunrise to sunset)
Suitability	Hiking, mountain biking, horseback riding
Usage	Low to moderate
Restrictions	Park permit required Pets must be on a leash
Nearest trailhead	Blue Mountain Trailhead Ramsay-Shockey Trailhead

The Shoshone Trail is located near Pinewood Lake in the Ramsay-Shockey Open Space. This 1.5 mile long trail is easy (66%) to moderate to hike. The closest access is from the Ramsay-Shockey Trailhead near the north end of the lake. A Larimer County Parks pass is required to use this trail. Take

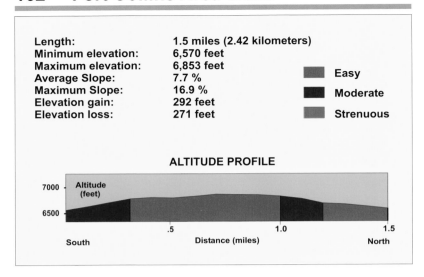

Length: 1.5 miles (2.42 kilometers)
Minimum elevation: 6,570 feet
Maximum elevation: 6,853 feet
Average Slope: 7.7 %
Maximum Slope: 16.9 %
Elevation gain: 292 feet
Elevation loss: 271 feet

■ Easy
■ Moderate
■ Strenuous

ALTITUDE PROFILE

the Besant Point Trail across the spillway and dam to the north end of the trail. There is a restroom here. The south end of

This bridge is for foot traffic only. Horsemen should take the side trail.

the trail is about a half mile away via the Besant Point Trail. At its south end, the Shoshone Trail leaves the Besant Point Trail and travels up a draw. It begins a moderate climb up the ridge to the west through a meadow with high grass. You get magnificent views of Pinewood Lake as you climb the ridge. Look for deer and elk in the high meadows early and late in the day. The trail makes a loop across the ridge, crossing a gulley over a foot bridge. Horsemen should cross the gulley just above the bridge. From here the trail makes a level path following an old road. You get good views of the lake from

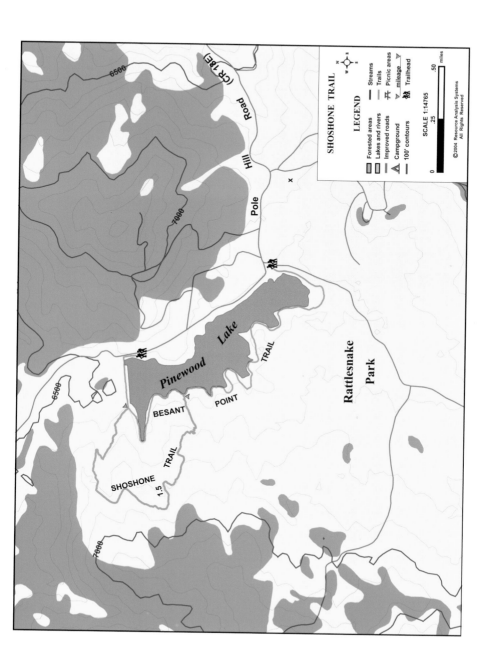

SHOSHONE TRAIL

LEGEND

Forested areas
Lakes and rivers
Improved roads
Campground
100' contours

Streams
Trails
Picnic areas
mileage
Trailhead

SCALE 1:14765

0   .25   .50   miles

©2004 Resource Analysis Systems
All Rights Reserved

6500

7000

6500

7000

Pinewood Lake

BESANT

POINT TRAIL

SHOSHONE

TRAIL

1.5

Rattlesnake
Park

Pole   Hill   Road

(CR 18E)

this area. The road ends at a fence line and the trail begins its descent back down to the lake. It makes several switchbacks

Look for deer and elk in these meadows in the early morning and evening hours.

as it travels down through a stand of ponderosa pine. There are good opportunities for viewing wildlife along this trail.

Directions:

The Shoshone Trail is located near Pinewood Lake. Take Highway 34 west from Loveland to County Road 29. Turn south on CR 29 and travel about two miles to CR 18E. Turn west on CR18E and travel about 6.7 miles to Pinewood Lake. The trail begins and ends from the Besant Point Trail. The closest trailhead is the Ramsay-Shocky Trailhead at the north end of the lake.

Length (one way)	7.14 miles (11.5 kilometers)
Elevation change	295 feet
Difficulty	Easy
Season	All year
Suitability	Hiking, biking, roller blading
Usage	High
Restrictions	Pets must be on a leash
Nearest trailhead	Cottonwood Glen Park Rolland Moore Park Edora Park

The Spring Creek Trail is a paved bike and hiking trail that travels from west to east Fort Collins following Spring Creek. This 7.1 mile long trail gradually loses 264 feet in elevation from west to east. It begins at Cottonwood Glen Park and winds around to the northeast, intersecting the Poudre

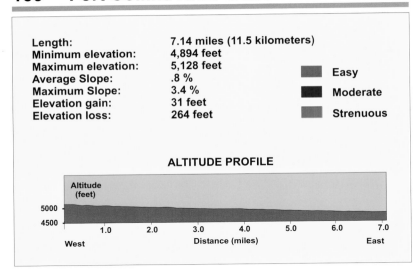

Length: 7.14 miles (11.5 kilometers)
Minimum elevation: 4,894 feet
Maximum elevation: 5,128 feet
Average Slope: .8 %
Maximum Slope: 3.4 %
Elevation gain: 31 feet
Elevation loss: 264 feet

Easy
Moderate
Strenuous

ALTITUDE PROFILE

River Trail on its eastern end. The trail leaves Cottonwood Glen Park and travels between housing areas before crossing under Taft Hill Road. It continues along side of houses and horse pastures and then crosses under Drake Road. From here it travels around Rolland Moore Park and passes under Shields Street. There are several ponds and impoundments

The trail travels under most busy streets.

of Spring Creek along its path where you'll see a variety of species of ducks and geese. The trail continues east and northeast passing under Center, College, Stuart, Stover, Lemay, Timberline, and Prospect streets.   Part of the trail travels through Edora Park. It intersects the Poudre River Trail about a half mile after passing under Prospect. There are air stations

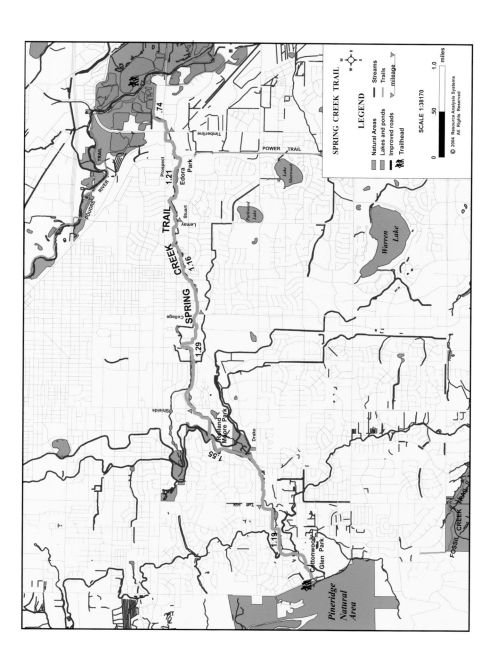

at a few places along the trail. This trail is easy to hike or ride. There are numerous access points all along its path, allowing

The Spring Creek Trail passes along side of the Spring Park Natural Area.

you to walk, run, or ride as far as you want.

Directions:

The Spring Creek Trail is located in the city of Fort Collins. Its primary access points are at Cottonwood Glen Park, Rolland Moore Park, and Edora Park. Take Drake Road west to Overland Trail. Turn south on Overland Trail to Cottonwood Glen Park. Take Drake Road west to Shields. Turn north on Shields and drive a short distance to Rolland Moore Park. Take S. Lemay Ave. to Stuart. Turn east on Stuart to Edora Park.

Length (one way)	3.13 miles (5.04 kilometers)
Elevation change	297 feet
Difficulty	Easy
Season	All year
Suitability	Hiking, mountain biking, horseback riding
Usage	Low to moderate
Restrictions	Park permit required Pets must be on a leash
Nearest trailhead	North Pines Trailhead South Shore Trailhead

The Sundance Trail is located near Carter Lake in the foothills west of Loveland. The trail is about 3.1 miles long and follows the west shore of Carter Lake. It can be accessed on the north from the North Pines Trailhead and on the south from the South Shore Trailhead. The trail is reasonably level

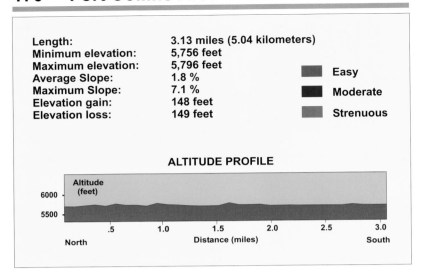

Length:	3.13 miles (5.04 kilometers)
Minimum elevation:	5,756 feet
Maximum elevation:	5,796 feet
Average Slope:	1.8 %
Maximum Slope:	7.1 %
Elevation gain:	148 feet
Elevation loss:	149 feet

■ Easy
■ Moderate
■ Strenuous

ALTITUDE PROFILE

except where it crosses a few gullies. Most of the trail travels just inside a stand of ponderosa pine trees. The majority of the trail surface is rocky except for the southern end. The southern quarter mile of the trail is wheelchair-accessible. This fine gravel surface leads to a small picnic area at the back of a large cove. You get great views of the lake and have access

The trail travels across several gullies like this along the western shore of Carter Lake.

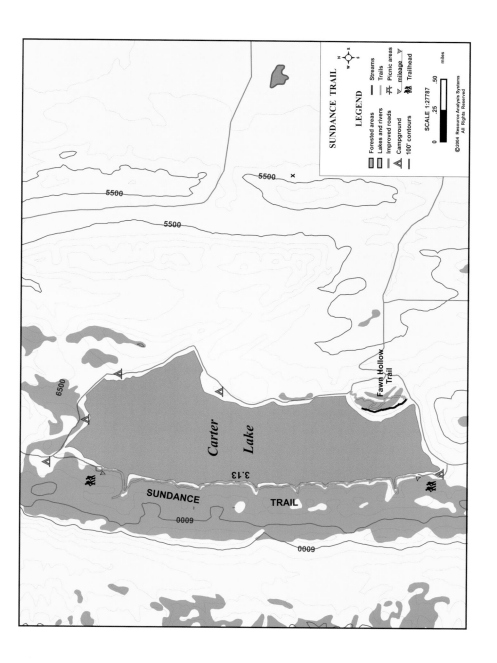

to fishing all along its length. This is a good trail for a shuttle hike where a vehicle is parked at both ends. A Larimer County

Here the trail climbs out of a gulch through some ponderosa pines.

Parks Pass is required to use this trail.

Directions:

The Sundance Trail is located near Carter Lake. Take Highway 34 west from Loveland to County Road 29. Turn south on CR 29 and travel about two miles to CR 18E. Turn west on CR18E and go about 2.2 miles to the entrance to Carter Lake. A fee is required to park at the trailhead. Turn right at the North Pines Road and take it to the trailhead.

Length (one way)	5.02 miles (8.08 kilometers)
Elevation change	1,226 feet
Difficulty	Easy
Season	All year
Suitability	Hiking, mountain biking, horseback riding
Usage	Moderate
Restrictions	Pets must be on a leash No camping within 1/4 mile
Nearest trailhead	Young Gulch Trailhead

The Young Gulch Trail begins from a large parking area just off Highway 14 across from the Ansel Watrous Campground. This trail travels up Young and Prairie gulches for about five miles where it ends at private property just short of the Stove Prairie Road. The trail is wide and well marked. It follows two streams up the bottom of the gulches, crossing them more than 30 times. It is almost impossible to avoid

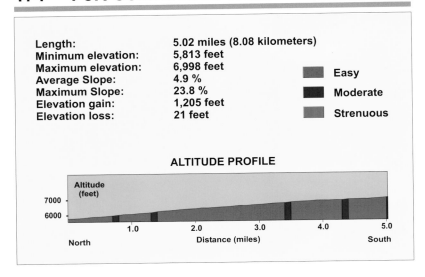

Length:	5.02 miles (8.08 kilometers)
Minimum elevation:	5,813 feet
Maximum elevation:	6,998 feet
Average Slope:	4.9 %
Maximum Slope:	23.8 %
Elevation gain:	1,205 feet
Elevation loss:	21 feet

Easy

Moderate

Strenuous

ALTITUDE PROFILE

Altitude
(feet)

7000

6000

1.0   2.0   3.0   4.0   5.0

North   Distance (miles)   South

getting your feet wet if you are hiking. The trail climbs about 1,200 feet in five miles. It is a very gradual climb and almost seems level. It winds up the gulch through beautiful stands of cottonwoods and ponderosa pine trees, interspersed with lush grassy meadows. Wild flowers are abundant in the spring.

The trail is wide at the beginning and easy to hike.

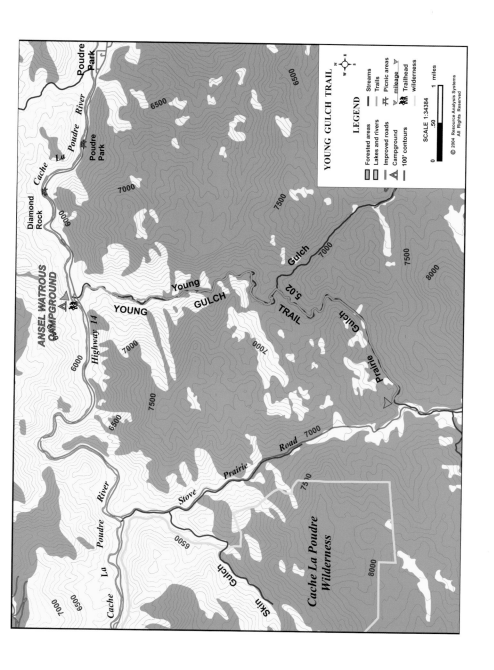

YOUNG GULCH TRAIL

LEGEND

Forested areas
Lakes and rivers
Improved roads
Campground
100' contours

Streams
Trails
Picnic areas
mileage
Trailhead
wilderness

SCALE 1:34384

0   .50   1 miles

Except for the stream crossings, this trail is of low difficulty. Fires and camping are prohibited within a quarter mile of the trail. For all practical purposes these activities are eliminated

Beautiful meadows surrounded by ponderosa pine make a great spot for a picnic.

because of the width and the steepness of the sides of the gulch. You would have to climb out of the gulch to get the required distance away. However, there are many beautiful spots to picnic.

Directions:

The Young Gulch Trail is located in Poudre Canyon. Take Highway 287 north from Fort Collins to La Porte. Continue on 287 north to Highway 14. Travel west on 14 for 12 miles to the trailhead. The trailhead is on the left hand side of the highway, just across from the Ansel Watrous Campground.

Index

Arthur's Rock 100, 101, 107, 109, 111, 118

Arthur's Rock Trail 100-102, 107, 111, 118, 119, 129, 130, 132

Audra Culver Trail 56-58

Besant Point Trail 17-20, 162, 164

Big Thompson River 134, 157

Black Powder Trail 21-24

Boyd Lake State Park 133, 134, 136

Carey Springs Trail 59, 60, 71

Carter Lake 33, 36, 169, 172

Cathy Fromme Natural Area 41-44

Coyote Ridge Natural Area 25

Coyote Ridge Trail 25-28

Devil's Backbone Open Space 29

Devil's Backbone Trail 29-32

Difficulty 16

East Valley Trail 103-105

Fawn Hollow Trail 33-36

Foothills Trail 37-40

Fossil Creek Trail 41-44

Gateway Mountain Park 21, 24

Greyrock Mountain 45, 46

Greyrock Trail 45-48

Herrington Trail 60, 61-63, 72, 75, 78, 81, 85, 89, 90

Hewlett Gulch Trail 49-52

Homestead Picnic Area 109, 111, 124, 131

Horsetooth Falls 64, 82

Horsetooth Falls Trail 64-66, 83, 85

Horsetooth Mountain Park 53-55, 56, 58, 59, 60, 61, 63, 64, 66, 67, 70, 72-74, 76, 78, 79, 81, 82, 85, 88, 91, 94, 106, 115, 117

Horsetooth Reservoir 38, 53, 58, 60, 63, 66, 68-70, 72, 74, 75, 77, 78, 81, 84, 87, 89, 90, 96, 100, 102, 104, 105, 109, 112, 118, 120, 123, 126, 129, 153, 156

Horsetooth Rock 53, 56, 57, 61, 68, 89, 90, 94, 95

Horsetooth Rock Trail 67-69, 82, 83, 96

Keyhole 30, 32

Loggers Trail 59, 60, 63, 70-72, 74, 75, 78, 80, 81

Lory State Park 53, 73, 75, 76, 78, 97-99, 100, 103, 106, 108, 109, 111, 112, 114, 117, 118, 120

Loveland Recreation Trail 133-136

Masonville Valley 56, 57, 94, 95
Meadow Trail 46, 48
Mill Creek Canyon 74
Mill Creek Link Trail 75, 100, 106-108
Mill Creek Trail 70, 73-75, 106, 107
Nomad Trail 76-78
Overlook Trail 24, 100, 101, 109-111, 125, 126
Park Trail 137, 138
Pineridge Natural Area 137-140
Pinewood Lake 17, 20, 161, 162, 164
Pleasant Valley Trail 141-144
Poudre Canyon 21, 22, 48, 52, 176
Poudre Park 49, 52
Poudre River 45, 48, 49, 52, 145, 146, 148, 149
Poudre River Bluffs 150, 152
Poudre River Trail 145-148, 149-152, 166
Power Trail 153-156
Ramsay-Shockey Open Space 161
Reservoir Trail 137, 140
Ridge Trail 137, 138
Rimrock Open Space Area 25, 26
Round Mountain Trail 157-160

Sawmill Trail 78, 79-81, 89
Seaman Reservoir 21, 24
Shoreline Trail 112-114
Shoshone Trail 18, 161-164
Soderberg Trail 60, 63, 65-67, 69, 72, 75, 78, 81, 82-84, 85, 87, 90, 93, 96
Soldier Canyon Falls 121-122
South Loop Trail 137, 138
South Valley Trail 76, 78, 108, 115-117
Spring Creek Trail 60-63, 65, 72, 74, 75, 78, 81, 82, 84, 85-87, 90, 91, 93, 165-168
Stout Trail 62, 81, 88-90
Summit Trail 46, 48
Sundance Trail 169-172
Timber Trail 100, 102, 118-120, 127, 129, 130, 132, 137, 138
Trail summary 12-15
Valley Trail 137, 138
Viewpoint Trail 137, 140
Waterfall Trail 121-123
Wathen Trail 85, 91-93
Well Gulch Trail 109, 111, 118, 124-126
West Valley Trail 100, 125, 130-132
Westridge Trail 74, 85, 86, 94-96, 118, 127-129
Young Gulch Trail 173-176

A CD ROM version is available to purchasers of this book for a nominal shipping and handling charge of $5.00. In addition to all of the information contained in this book, the CD also contains printable trail maps and directions and 150 additonal trail photos. It also includes descriptions, photos, and directions to the currently open City of Fort Collins Natural Areas. This easy to use CD has the capability to search for trails based on:

> Trail difficulty
> Trail suitability
> Trails within Horsetooth Mountain Park
> Trails within Lory State Park
> All trails alphabetically

Send $5.00 to:

> RAS Publishing
> 2917 Eagle Drive
> Fort Collins, CO 80526

Make checks payable to RAS Publishing.

Check out other RAS Publishing offerings:

Colorado Campgrounds: Volume 1 - Poudre Canyon & Red Feather Lakes

Colorado's Indian Peaks Wilderness - A Guide To Trails And Lakes

Leaving The Crowds Behind - A Guide To Backcountry Camping In Rocky Mountain National Parks

Rocky Mountain Trails - A Complete Guide To Trails In Rocky Mountain National Park

For more information on these books and CD, log on to:

www.resourceanalysis.com

or call: 970-226-2311